DOGS IN VESTS

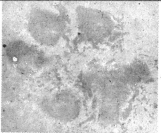

Mazie

MIRIAM RICHARD, VICTOR FADOOL & KARIS LADEWIG

EMOTIONAL SUPPORT **SERVICE DOG IN TRAINING** SERVICE DOG

EMPOWERING NARRATIVES OF FAMILIES RAISING, TRAINING, & PARTNERING WITH SERVICE ANIMALS

Dogs In Vests: Empowering Narratives of Families Raising, Training, & Partnering with Service Dogs

by Miriam Richard, Victor Fadool, and Karis Ladewig

ISBN: 978-0-692-09877-6

This book is the author's story of how she and those in her community came together to raise two allergen detection and medical alert dogs, one for her family and one for a deserving family in her community. This is not a comprehensive training manual. The information enclosed is for educational and supportive purposes only. The author and publisher cannot be held accountable for any adverse reactions or consequences that may occur as a result of utilizing the information in this book. This is not a stand alone complete resource. Always utilize a certified trainer to help you implement a program for your service dog's individual needs.

This book was written as a resource guide with our personal narratives as to how we came to know this information.

To be as candid as possible, some names of the involved parties have been changed to protect their privacy.

To contact the author, visit www.dogsinvests.com and *Facebook* page (Medical Alert and Allergen Detection) Dogs in Vests.

REVIEWS

I learned so much from this book. It served as great conversation with my co-workers. I mentioned a couple of occurrences with my dog, Jaxx, and told them how interesting and applicable it was to my life. We discussed our pets and how we could train our service animals with the methods in this book.

"Building that trust is more important at first than teaching your dog to sit. It's not just trust, it's also confidence you are building in your dog, yourself and techniques." This information is golden.

I can't wait to apply these things to my precious Jaxx and realizing in some situations why he reacted the way he has. I giggled a lot while reading about Victor's misfortune because I can relate so well to the little bit of everything being destroyed. I loved this book!

— Danielle Casarez

I could feel the authors passion and dedication, while reading Dogs In Vests. I found it captivating compared to reading a regular training guide and learned interesting things about service and allergen training that I didn't know.

— David Hillie DMV

I thoroughly enjoyed reading this book! It was hard for me to put it down! I was moved by the journey of the characters. Who would have thought that reading a book about service dogs would be so inspiring?! I am so impressed with the authors ability to com-municate the importance and value of a service dog.

This book is so well written that I felt the authors compassion for the characters. I was deeply touched by the story of the Ladewig family. It broke my heart to know that the Ladewig children suffered different illnesses but what joy I felt when Mazie entered their lives! Mazie brought such healing to their spirits and contentment to their hearts. It's amazing what proper training of a service dog can do! It could save the life of a sick child. Priceless!

Lastly, I'm so happy that the authors allowed us to view the world through Mazie's eyes. It was so funny! I want to see Mazie's story in an animated film! I love Mazie! She's my new hero!

— Sheila Bickham

I loved the book and read every word when I received it today. Hopefully this new book will bring education and assistance to many. Thank you for sharing.

— Carole Hamill

Dogs in Vests is a wonderful look into the life of not only a service dog, but the people they serve. As humans I believe we continually underes-timate the ability of our furry friends, but this book shows just how truly remarkable and intelligent dogs can be. I highly recommend reading about these incredible dogs, their handlers, and their life saving journey.

Having seen Stella work in a public and distracting setting, and do so at a very high level I encourage you to read this book knowing that these dogs do what they do with lives on the line.

Dogs in Vests is an incredible opportunity to help the families in our communities per-severe through situations most of us can't begin to imagine. I hope you read this book and finish it as inspired as I am!

— Kierin Stevens

Coming from someone who has paid to have their service dog trained, Dogs in Vests is a phenomenal guide for anyone interested in learning what training your own service dog entails. I wish I had had access to this information three years ago.

— Stephen Ellis

Dogs in Vests opened my eyes to service dogs. Before reading, I was not aware of the great mental and physical health benefits they can provide to individuals on a day to day basis to help make someone's life easier and more enjoyable. Thanks to Dogs in Vests am more informed and some very deserving people are getting some furry friends added to their family (:

— Abby Speight

I must say, your vulnerability in telling this story is tremendously powerful. It really adds a deep dimension that I was not expecting and sucked me into the story. Nice work!!!

— Stratton L. Ladewig, Ph.D.

ACKNOWLEDGEMENTS

An incredible special thanks is extended to all who have supported me on this journey of raising and training dogs for the writing of this book. I am forever grateful for my best friend and husband, Mike Richard, and our three children who believe in my endeavors and lovingly put up with early morning dog chores and the chaos of three dogs in the house.

I could not have written the book without my dear friend and editor, Linda Savage, who is willing to work with my scattered ideas and help guide me until they come together as I had envisioned.

I am grateful for my cowriters and contributors Victor Fadool, Karis Ladewig, Megan Ladewig, Katelyn Richard, Ilester Little, Jennifer Ladewig, Mason Richard, James Richard, along with Amy Novacek and McKinley Novacek, who all make the story come to life with their stories.

Lastly, I am honored to work with these amazing pups! Also, I appreciate working with various trainers, namely, Valerie Fry, who believed in me and Stella, and Jillian Skalky, as well as those listed in the "Appendix." In addition, thanks to the above mentioned trainers as well as well as those that I contacted via media or by phone, who contributed to my understanding of the dog brain and teaching techniques.

I want to extend a special thanks to my final proofreaders, Regan Van Eaton and Stratton Ladewig, my photo editor, Harrison Scott, for polishing the final draft, and Jana Rade for formatting and cover design.

WE THANK GOD FOR ALL THE GOOD IN OUR LIVES.

TABLE OF CONTENTS

INTRODUCTION

S it. Shake. Come. Alert. Save my child's life. You know, just a few natural commands for any household pet, right? Would you do whatever it took to set up lines of defense that could aid in saving your child's life? That's what we did. The reward from introducing a service animal to our family has extended far beyond those first-hand alerts to/for ingredients that could induce anaphylaxis in my daughter, and the detection of foods that could prove toxically antagonizing for my son's auto-immune disease. It has become my passion to challenge others to embrace the reward, as well.

Our (and I am betting yours, too) first and probably best-known use of a dog in service to humans was for the sight impaired. Until recently, and for obvious health concerns, the only animals allowed in public places like grocery stores, restaurants, and on public transportation were 'Seeing Eye' dogs. Society is changing quickly, however, and proclaimed 'service animals' are popping up everywhere. You see them in the mall, in medical offices, on planes and buses, in Uber rides, and pretty much anywhere humans go. The importance of having an animal registered, trained, vaccinated, and insured goes highly understated. Spotting so many imposter service Animals walking around is embarrassing and disheartening. A woman was removed from an airline for having an unlicensed Emotional Support *peacock* (https://www.usatoday.com/story/travel/news/2018/01/30/artist-her-emotional-support-peacock-denied-entry-flight/1081098001/, accessed 15 April 2018.). Increasing reports of emotional support dogs acting aggressively and relieving themselves during a flight are also in the media. Fortunately, airlines are cracking down on the insanity people are trying to force upon the unsuspecting public.

Stella placing out of traffic at airport.

The silliness downplays the seriousness of a trained service animal, which is an expensive commitment. These animals are not just accessory pieces to our lives. They're animals that are trained to help those they serve avoid life threatening circumstances or improve quality of life for those with disabilities. Aside from the blind, service animals assist the deaf, elderly and handicapped; search and rescue teams; military and law enforcement; and those with invisible illnesses. We want you as the reader to have a better understanding, from a myriad of viewpoints, of what it looks like to raise and train a *true* service animal and the benefits that they bring everyone whose lives they touch. We also hope that we can broaden your vision of the type of aid a skilled dog can bring to supplement or even in some cases potentially replace current medical practices or complex medical problems.

Raising, training, and providing an incredible home for a service animal has become my life-changing hobby. It was born out of my love of domestic animals. Slowly, this evolved from the exciting bond of training my own puppy to a passion for training dogs for those who may not have the patience, finances, or ability to do it themselves. That being said, my hope is to guide *you* through the responsibility of raising a service animal in *your* family. There are vast differences between bringing home a young puppy to join the family and extending that initial training of stay, sit, and fetch verses alerting for allergens or other life-saving skills. Training of animals that 'help' varies depending on your needs. That's why it is critical to know the inherent differences among pet therapy, emotional support and service animals.

Pet therapy animals may be of many species and are trained to behave in pubic and in a manner that is supportive to the *emotional* needs of a person in their home, hospital, or nursing home. These animals are frequently seen as reading buddies to younger school age children or on college campuses to help with stress before exams. The legal extent that they can be in spaces occupied by humans is limited.

Emotional support animals are of a variety of species and do not have training requirements (herein lies the problem) but are allowed under the Housing Act to accompany a human into a variety of previously "off limits for animals" spaces. This includes free airline travel with a certified doctor's letter explaining why the person they are traveling with would need such an animal. By law, only two questions are allowed to be addressed to the animal's owner, whether it be by the airlines or any store owner or housing establishment, and those are: "Is this a service dog?" and "What task is the dog trained to do?" This, in my humble opinion, has resulted in too broad an interpretation of the laws and many people taking advantage of the system.

Under the federal Americans with Disabilities Act, service Animals can be dogs or miniature horses and are allowed rights and privileges. This gives them access to housing, air travel, and entrance into all public places the disabled person is allowed, provided the animal is *under control*. They should be trained and pass public access training tests and additional training that addresses a specific task that would not be natural for the animal to do without such training. The task must help to mitigate a specific limitation for the handler. Many accreditations have a higher standard and require the animal to be trained in two tasks, for example opening doors and picking up dropped items and returning to the handler.

Fearing lawsuits and negative publicity or discrimination charges, many public places including public transportation, retail owners, and restaurants feel their hands are tied when it comes to allowing animals access. Added to this challenge, websites exist that will provide letters for a fee without ever seeing a patient or animal.

However, airlines are implementing changes to deal with this issue. A documentation check of doctor letters is being considered by some airlines to weed out those passengers simply looking for a free way to transport their pet.

The biggest issue in jeopardy would be the blocking of all animals in public places, which would be a disaster to those who qualify for such a companion. These service animals could acquire a social stigma of being an imposter, demeaning both their true calling and the integrity of the humans they serve. Lastly, there is a serious safety issue to the unsuspecting public and to the service animals themselves. True service dogs are bred and trained to be docile and kind. This takes thousands of hours of training and likewise costs thousands of dollars. When confronted in a public place by an animal who is untrained and aggressive, the service dog may well shutdown in this encounter, resulting in the end of his career and loss of a valuable investment.

As you will read, in our personal journey, we moved from emotional to therapy to service training in considering how to best serve our family. At each step, knowing the costs, training regimens, and time required are important considerations. While I will discuss in length the process I took from beginning to end, why I did it, what various levels of service can be attained and passed forward, the human element perspective from the adults and children these dogs serve cannot be underemphasized. What a joy it has been to collaborate with friends who live with emotional support animals, trainers, and breeders who have a heart for others in this field, and with young authors who give fresh perspective from their budding eyes—and even the unique perspective of the puppies themselves. We want you to have a better understanding from a myriad of angles of what it looks like to raise a service animal and the benefits that they bring to everyone whose lives they touch.

Allow me to introduce you to those who shared our journey and their contributions:

The Jay and Amy Novacek are the breeders of the service dogs. Our initial dog, Stella, was from the first of four litters. Amy is well known in the equestrian world and has personally trained two service dogs for her own life-threatening medical conditions.

Valerie Fry is certified dog trainer and comes once a week to help me train Stella. She has worked extensively for a non-profit organization that provides service dogs for disabled veterans. She is working on her "training the trainer" manual she hopes to publish soon to help make service dogs more affordable to those who need them.

The Ladewig family: Three of their six children have intestinal failure, resulting in two of the three children needing feeding tubes and central access lines. They are on the search for non-medical alternatives to aid in the care and emotional support of their children. Mazie, our second trained puppy, was purchased specifically for this, her "Forever Family," and helps the children in a way medicine alone never could. The father of this family is in the Army Reserve and was mobilized for a year starting October 2017. It is our joy to publish the perspective of two young authors from this family, Karis, and Megan Ladewig.

My family, the Richard family, is training our own service dog Stella to alert us to food allergens. We also provided the initial training of another of the Novacek' puppies to give to the Ladewig Family. While the entire family contributes in their own irreplaceable way to the care and training of our dog, Katelyn writes here from her unique viewpoint as a young child that Stella was trained to serve. We have also included insights from other members of the family as to the impact a service animal has on young adults.

Victor, a friend, author, and local business owner who is guiding us through the technicalities of writing our story. Victor also happens to live with an emotional support dog. He brings insight from working at a premier dog park and cantina in the Dallas area.

Ilester started working on this project, actively filming, editing, training dogs, and helping put together our future website, while completing real estate classes. He was drawn to help upon learning the heart-warming story of the Ladewig family. He is writing his story through his awareness that a service dog might be a realistic option for those who struggle with mental illness.

CHAPTER 1

THE RANCH

We purchased our first Labradoodle from Amy almost completely by accident after meeting at a diabetes fundraiser that my husband and I attended in 2015. Amy had donated a dog to be bid on at auction. She disclosed that her hope was for someone to adopt their Labradoodle from the fundraiser and train her as a therapy animal—perhaps to visit kids in hospitals. Coincidently, my daughter's Social Skills teacher had recently shared that interacting and training a puppy would benefit my daughter's nonverbal social skills, and those skills would carry over into other social settings. Animals are great conversation starters. They serve as emotional support for anxiety surrounding social connection and create empathy awareness. What a fortuitous meeting! If WE adopted a dog, we could raise it as a therapy animal to benefit our nine-year-old daughter Katelyn.

MORE ON AMY NOVACEK

The Novacek lives on a ranch in Texas populated with pigs, buffalo, horses, and cattle. Over the years, she had many canine companions, but none compared to Nick, a sweet tempered, brown-sugar colored male Labradoodle. She was heartbroken when her beloved dog was tragically kicked and killed by a bull. Turning her heartache into action, Amy set about breeding a Poodle and a Lab to yield similar qualities of her Nick. Amy felt that Poodles are known as the second smartest dog, yet nimble on their back limbs and could literally stand up and hug you without knocking you over. She felt the Labs were healthy, low maintenance, very willing to work; they are known for easy trainability. Research and tenacity led her to terrific specimens of a male Poodle and female Lab, and she raised each from puppyhood. The Standard Poodle was a phantom named Bentley and had the qualities of a great pet therapy animal. The female, Bella, was a regal silver Lab, which was a yellow Labrador Retriever of sturdy stock with a protective family orientation. These two were her best hope, and once they turned three she would breed them.

In the years of waiting, Amy had no idea how her own life would change on a dime. One ordinary day as she pulled into her ranch driveway, she was rear-ended by a driver traveling 70 miles per hour, resulting in numerous injuries including eight broken bones. Additionally, the trauma from the accident overwhelmed her adrenal system and threw her into a life-threatening condition of adrenal insufficiency A.I. (see resources). The year of healing that ensued was tumultuous at best and involved agonizing rehabilitation appointments, and many days were best left in bed.

But the day came when Bella came into heat and was of age, so well-set plans must proceed. The most exciting day of the year was the delivery of 12 puppies—way to go Bella! She did need a C-section assist from the vet, but these were very healthy puppies, and all weighed a good 2–3 pounds. The highlights of Amy's days were going out to the kitchen and visiting with each sweet bundle of joy, watching out for

Bella while checking on her for signs of stress. She also put in place a camera to check on the litter if she needed to attend to the horses or other animals on the ranch. Amy placed the whelping box area just outside the bedroom for easy monitoring as she still had much recovering to do. These sweet pups were raised in the kitchen and living room of the house and became socialized to humans rapidly.

As the pups got older, Amy and her daughter, McKinley, searched diligently to identify which pup would be their personal Labradoodle, one Amy could use as a pet therapy dog because they attended many charity events involving children. A dog would brighten a child's day. She and her daughter took turns sneaking each pup into her bed to spend the night and each got a shower and a ride in the car. At five weeks, she had whittled her selection down to three: two boys and a girl.

At the same time, Amy put a pup up for auction at *Racing for the Stars* where she met Miriam Richard. The pup did not come to the event, but a larger than life poster was displayed. The pup's vet was also available to answer any questions about the puppies along with their parent's health histories.

Daily the family got on the floor and played with the pups, but admittedly Amy spent just a bit more time with her favorites. As a result, they started to have a favoring toward her as well. One morning, something completely out of the ordinary happened. The little pup she had named Hank started to lick Amy incessantly on her hand in a way she thought quite odd. It was not an everyday occurrence; however, the pup returned to this behavior over and over. It wasn't until the third or fourth time this happened Amy correlated the licking with the fact that she was feeling quite awful. Her adrenal medicine needed adjustment. OH! MY goodness! Hank had been alerting her all along—naturally alerting dog! How fortuitous! Not only were the pups an emotional support, prompting her to get out of bed on those super challenging days, now one was saving her life. This single incident prompted Amy to expand her vision of dogs not only used for emotional and therapeutic uses but breeding service dogs specific to invisible diseases. It was a wonderful time to be connected with

Miriam, whose own processes would lead her to eventually train one from this litter as a service dog for her family.

MCKINLEY NOVACEK

I spent time with the puppies from day one. I play with them the second they can move about. It's exciting to see the small puppies grow up and become such loving and loyal dogs.

Of course, there is a lot of responsibility with raising the puppies. I help take care of them, keeping one or two in my room in a crate at night so they won't feel uncomfortable when they must be crate trained in their new homes.

I also work with them on leash and harness, teaching them basic commands. When they are ready to go to their new homes, they will know how to sit and lie down and will be completely familiar with a leash.

MIRIAM'S FLASHBACK

My favorite childhood memory of all time is waking up on Christmas at 6 A.M. to a box that was covered in red puppy paper. It was open on the top, and inside was the smallest black Toy Poodle that was no bigger than my palm. At 8 years-old, I could dream of nothing better than to have my very own Toy Poodle puppy.

I had a hamster, and the family Beagle, who was getting older and was stubborn, unwilling to learn my commands "slow," "go," and "no"—words I had been working on during our walks, if you could call them that. I just kept being pulled at a record pace when the deceptively lazy Beagle suddenly came to life chasing after squirrels willy-nilly. A fresh new start with a darling pup was more than welcome.

We formed a bond unlike any other. This puppy was so smart, and I was able to take her with me everywhere and dress her up as my live dolly. She became my little audience when I played teacher.

Buddy and Hank pose with Amy Novacek.

In fact, she was my best pupil, outsmarting all my other dolls. Muffin always had the right answer and put her paw up when asked to raise her hand (shake).

Muffin was my biggest fan. When I would play the lead in my backyard musicals or play preacher in my playhouse and give sermons, she watched intently. She always enjoyed being dressed up, taken for a stroll in my toy baby carriage, and paraded around the neighborhood.

One of my favorite memories was the Fourth of July parade in which I was Wonder Woman, and Muffin was Wonder Dog. By this time, her multiple tricks included sit, speak, shake, and turn—which she displayed by standing on back legs like a true circus dog (in my dreams we were famous)—lie down, and roll over. With our costumes handmade by my grandmother and myself, we were the stars of the parade that year.

Muffin and I experienced great adventures. We had the family lake house where she learned to swim to the ladder, hang on to the rung, and wait until somebody came to rescue her on the dock. She would hold her hand of cards at the table, sitting upright with pillows propping her left and right sides. She would always have her cards ready for Crazy 8, with never a worry that she would be caught cheating.

Muffin was there for me during some really tough years. The pain of experiencing learning differences compounded with a slight facial nasal flattening and heavy eyelids provided perfect targets for my bullying peers. I added to my plight by reporting to the administration that my entire class had cheated on a test. I'm convinced that truth-tellers and those with perceived differences have a special place in God's heart. Daily remarks were carelessly tossed at me about my looks with *"Chinese Eyes,"* *"Hong Kong Phooey,"* and *"Chink"* being the most common phrases. I was shunned by my peers at lunch to the point of having to sit with the younger grades. All of this resulted in coming home daily in tears to the only one I felt really understood me, my little dog. During miserable fifth, sixth, and seventh grades, she was without a doubt my best friend on earth, my guardian angel.

As I got older and started dating, the first family member the young man would be introduced to was my beloved angel, and if she didn't like them, they were out. Poodles can live for up to 20 years I would let them know, and she and I would always be family.

Sweet Muffin did live until I was 24 and passed just after my wedding. When she had gone blind and her world had shrunk, her very favorite place was that little bitty toy baby carriage from her puppy days where she would lie on her back, reassured and safe.

CHAPTER 2

ADOPTING STELLA

BACK ON THE RANCH

It was so much fun to go out to the Novacek ranch and play with twelve puppies born in that first litter. We were also able to meet both Bella and Bentley. Although we were on board with the idea of a puppy, I had been firm with my daughter that this was a preliminary visit—that we may not take a puppy from the first litter we viewed. After all, our nine-year-old yellow Lab, Chloe, was still active, and we weren't sure we wanted two dogs at one time. We hadn't raised a puppy in over twenty years, and I remember our first dog, Bailey, was a tremendous amount of work during the first two years it took to train her properly. I did recall that all that work paid off as she turned into a stellar dog who would follow two step commands: getting a named object and delivering it to a specific person. Funny what you can do with your extra time before children. Now I had three children and less time, so we were seriously considering this whole idea to see if we wanted a puppy from this litter.

The majority of the puppies were incredibly laid back, and being raised in the home within the family's main living area meant lots of human interaction. One in particular let me flip her on her back, mess with her ears, pinch her paws, and check for startle response, play drive, and food drive. This puppy passed all my tests. I was so impressed with the breeding and demeanor of the puppies that, although I did not know if we needed a puppy at this time, here we were with a puppy that we could not pass up. That is how Stella-Rosa (her name was selected while she was sleeping on her back under the wine cabinet) came to live with us. We were the first to adopt from that litter and were able to take her home that day. The Novaceks showed signs of great breeders. They called the next day to make sure I cared for their puppy properly and quizzed me on how many ounces of water I had given her. I was also asked to send photos, so they could see how she was adapting. They are so conscientious that they even said that if we could not keep or handle the puppy for any reason that we should bring her directly back to them.

I knew Amy was hoping we would train the pup to become a therapy dog. But what did I know about training a therapy dog? How did that differ from raising a pet? My prior training experience would be considered intermediate at best and was from 20 years ago. I wanted to leverage what experience I had from years ago and incorporate it with up-to-date teaching methodology. Our previous trainer had kept up with those techniques and was willing to come within two days. Low and behold, I was surprised to find out that all training had changed from correction to positive reinforcement. I had a lot to learn!

Miriam and Katelyn pick up Stella-Rosa.

CHAPTER 2: ADOPTING STELLA

CHAPTER 3

THE TRAINING OF STELLA

Stella thrived under the newer techniques right out of the gate. She quickly learned how to fetch, let go, where her crate was located and its primary purpose. All of this occurred at nine weeks old. Even though this breed is known for their intellect and capacity to be helpful, I was still shocked at the speed upon which she picked up commands.

Early on in Stella's training, our trainer suggested that we log onto a site that specializes in hunting and basic positive obedience training in order to begin follow-up training from home (www. leerburg.com; see resources). It was exceptionally fun to watch the videos with Stella, who as a little puppy would watch and follow along with all the other puppies on the screen. She essentially would train with me.

One month into training Stella, one of my sons started having various gastrointestinal complications, experiencing extreme pain, and he was undergoing multiple visits to the emergency room. This definitely helped us home in on our training for Stella to be trained as a therapy animal. When licensed, she would be able to come not only into the hospital, but colleges, schools, and nursing homes. Having Stella as comfort would be a distraction from the pain my son was enduring while waiting for approval to take pain medication, which often was several hours. Our online research led us to Pet Partners (see resources). We followed their protocol and trained Stella to their standards.

The next step was to figure out the primary venue in which our dog would be working and determine additional prerequisites. When looking at the requirements for therapy animals at the hospital to which my son was frequently admitted, I found out that this hospital, as well as various others in the area, already had contracts with specific therapy animal providers. Time was of the essence, and it appeared there was too much red tape to get through before getting accepted into a program that would give Stella an opportunity to work with my son in the hospital.

Could we take-another-tact entirely? My daughter was a friend with our neighbor's daughter, Christy. I shared carpool duties with her mother over the years, and the girls had class together. But it was our puppy and Christy's major medical issues surrounding food allergies that brought us together. On one of her emergency room visits, we learned her parents had brought their service-dog-in-training to the hospital. What had they done to get to the point where they could bring Christy's dog to the hospital? What goes into training service dogs verses therapy animals? Up to this point, I did not realize you could train a dog to alert to food allergies. Could this potentially keep my son out of the hospital altogether? The idea of having a personal family pet that can keep my family members out of the hospital by alerting to food allergens and potentially provide joy and comfort as a therapy animal to other patients in need sounded delightful. Onward and upward to the next level of training as a medically approved working service dog!

TRAINING FOR ALLERGENS

With this new approach in mind, we had to find someone who was able to help us with scent work. Stella, at five months, was well trained for basic obedience on outings at this point but hadn't focused on allergy detection. Finding qualified professionals was tough because most people did not specialize in these areas. (It is relatively new—about ten years in the making—so there are very few trainers skilled in this quickly developing area.) And if they did, they were extremely expensive and hard to come by. Our neighbor's trainer was three and a half hours away in Houston. The training is rigorous and somewhat exploratory, depending on the allergy. We were blessed with a reference from our veterinarian. We welcomed Valerie into our home.

Valerie has had years of training experience and holds a multitude of training certifications. She has experience in training with a disabled veterans program, traditional scent work, and what was required of a service dog for public access. Valerie had not specifically done allergen detection, but from a training standpoint, she felt she could help us move forward using traditional scent work and the specifics of what was required of a service animal to pass their public access exam. The more she worked with Stella, the more she felt our puppy had the intelligence to train as not only a pet therapy animal but also excel as an allergen detecting service dog. She had us work on traditional scent tasks like hide a treat under one of three cones and play "Find It," a version of the shell game. One of our favorite training games allowed Katelyn and her friends to play. They hid up to 20 treats throughout the main living and kitchen area and sent Stella on a "search." In addition, one or more children would hide with a generous quantity of treats and they would play *hide and seek* with Stella, helping the searching child. This was great fun for everyone. Where we all grew the most was when I discovered the most effective way to gently move Stella forward when progress seemed thwarted. We learned dogs don't generalize well and that even initial training steps must be broken down into micro steps.

Stella learns scent with cone games.

BREAKING IT DOWN

One area of training that required broken-down steps was in teaching Stella how to shut objects, like a door in the home. First, we put a sticky note on our hand and told her "touch." When she mastered "touch," we progressed to "push touch," which was having her touch our hand with her nose. And we would give resistance or over-pressure back at her nose to mimic the weight of a door, and then give her a treat. Next, we put the sticky note on the door and asked her to "push touch." At first, we just opened the door an inch, so that very little pressure would cause the door to close and she would be successful. As she progressed, we opened the door further and further expecting a better effort, encouraging more, with a treat reward. Eventually, Stella got to the point where, when the door was open, we could tell her to "shut the door" (we started to exaggerate the SH sound and said, "puSH touch SHut" for a month), and she would push touch it closed. A month after she was able to push the door shut, we moved

10 feet away and gave the same command. It took another two months, but eventually Stella learned to shut the door on her own without us standing there or yelling from across the room. Consistency is key when linking actions. Every action needs to be repeated every time she opens or closes the door.

The next task of course would be to open the door. We called it "tug" because of the style of door handles we have that are like levers requiring one to push down and pull the door open. Stella had already learned "tug" with a tug-o-war game. That made it easy and fun for her (and us) to understand the command while she learned the task. We used a dog toy on a rope that people use for fetch and hung it from the door handle. We would have her stand at the door and tell her "tug," and when she'd pull on the toy, the lever would go down and the door would open. She quickly made the connection that she could open the door from the inside this way and let herself outside. Hanging the toy from this specific handle also taught Stella not to jump up on the door to open it. She could simply bite the toy and pull to open from the inside and bite the toy and pull shut from the outside. For this to work well, you need to have a tug on both sides of the door. This task literally *opened up doors* for us to make other tasks easier to grasp and conceptualize for Stella.

Please understand that this does not come easy. Training any animal requires a lot of time, energy, and patience. Daily, repetitive commands and short, fun, training sessions using 3–5 rep's multiple times per day while adding in duration, distance, and distraction as appropriate make for success. The goal is to make it a game and as fun and enjoyable as possible for both you and your dog.

We focused on various similar tasks throughout the first nine months so that Stella could pass the K-9 Good Citizen Test that Valerie recommended in order to be an official service animal-in-training. What that means in our state is that Stella can go anywhere that her handler/trainer is allowed. Up to this point we were not taking her in public unless the locations were dog friendly facilities such as Home Depot, Lowes, or outdoor dining facilities.

Mazie watching intently as Stella models opening
a drawer to retrieve a bag of treats.

CHAPTER 4

THE LADEWIG CONNECTION

L ife, of course, moved ahead at top speed during Stella's training. We were in and out of the hospital handling our son's health complications, working, and generally managing a household. We have been blessed when going through something tough or traumatic—to notice those people walking along a similar path and are able to reach out, bond, comfort, and support one another. So, it is really no surprise that we developed a close relationship with the Ladewig Family. Stratton and Jennifer are incredible parents to six amazing children, including the two eldest girls 19 and 15, a boy 14, followed by Karis 12, Megan 8, and the youngest Phoebe 6 (at the time we met). Each of the children is afflicted by a genetic condition called dysautonomia. This means that the autonomic nervous system has gone awry. The autonomic nervous system regulates heart rate, blood pressure, and digestion, just to name a few of the main responsibilities. Some are affected more than others, causing financial and emotional hardships for this amazing family. My whole family, especially my husband Mike could not believe the intensity of the challenges this family faced.

I originally met Jennifer and her daughters at a meeting for a mission trip to Guatemala. It was a divine appointment. Within the year, Jennifer and I found out that we had a lot in common as mothers, specifically involving our family dynamics and various health complications and anaphylactic food allergies. Her children spent extended time in the hospital more times than she could count, and our lives were beginning to be consumed similarly by hospital visits and research. It was an intense dive into a world that seemed to throw limitless information, research, laboratory tests, and results our way with no easy solutions. We both were looking for something to help ease the burden on our kids and family members.

During the summer months, we hired the eldest Ladewig daughter, to house-sit and dog-watch. She loved spending time with the pup, spoiling and playing mommy to the dog daily. Growing up, she was told that a dog wasn't an option due in part to the allergies the dander flared in two of her siblings and the hectic unpredictable life that came with the medical issues from which they suffered. Upon arriving home from each trip, we learned that as many of the family members that were able came and spent time doting on Stella, the sweet energetic puppy, and Chloe, the lovable lab. To our surprise, it seemed all did well with Stella due to her coat being more Poodle-like and a few of the children could even spend the night and not have issues if they took a Benadryl and washed their hands thoroughly after petting Chloe. My daughter, Katelyn, got along so well with three of the Ladewig girls whom she is sandwiched by in age that we started having bi-monthly playdates and gatherings.

Around Christmas time, I noticed that Jennifer was having a particularly stressful day and she cuddled with Stella (now 9 and a half months) and then sidled up beside Chloe who was on the floor. She just sat and visited, talking with the girls and me, and before we knew it she was in a better mood. I noticed she had been on the floor for over an hour and a half enjoying the company of the dogs.

In my health coach kind of way, I asked Jennifer if she ever had a dog. She said she did as a child but that it just wasn't in the cards with all the kid's immunosuppression issues and allergies. I asked her to dream big and ponder whether the joy of having a pup AND the more recently discovered fact that some bacteria can be helpful AND the latest statistics on kids who grow up with dogs usually have less asthma might mean a new addition to the house. Could she see a future in which a service dog perhaps might lessen the burden of care duties and offer respite in small increments on those very difficult days?

CHAPTER 5

KARIS

SPRING OF 2017

During one hospital stint for the Ladewig daughter, Karis, I decided to bring our now service dog-in-training, Stella, up to the hospital. She had just passed her Canine Good Citizen certification. As a service dog-in-training in the state of Texas, the law states the dog is allowed to go where handler and trainer can go. Stella was still a puppy at this point, just around one year old.

When we took her to visit Karis in the hospital, we found the time they spent together to be incredibly successful for both Stella and Karis. We could just see the positive energy exchange between the two and both instinctively knew their roles. It was as if Stella knew she was there to lift Karis's spirits, which was evident by the smile that beamed across her face and the lilt in her voice. Apparently, dogs are very good at reading nonverbal mannerisms.

Karis knew she was helping Stella feel important and needed, as well. Both just basked in each other's affections for the duration of the visit. It was such a beautiful site to witness. Healing, at least of the spirit, was taking place before our very eyes. Stella was asked to come back to visit three more times.

Karis returned home playing catch-up for her school courses and processing the previous months of hospitalization. It wasn't long before the emotional and physical roller coaster took its toll and Karis become disheartened and despondent, wanting simply to indulge in the simple pleasure everyone else calls food. She remembered the sweet savory delectable delight of a Krispy Creme donut that Tim Hawkins describes as "eating a baby angel of goodness in his youtube comedy shows. (3Nails1Cross4Given. "Tim Hawkins on Krispy Kreme." YouTube, YouTube, 7 Nov. 2015, www.youtube.com/watch?v=NAlvaZzq23k.) She couldn't resist when she found a box in the family kitchen. Unfortunately, when you are diagnosed with complete intestinal failure, the outcome is less than angelic, landing her back yet again in the emergency room, dangerously close to death and readmitted for an extended stay. During this time, Stella went to visit every 5–7 days.

Mere days after Karis returned home, I found myself invited to go on a full day tour of the newest Star Stadium. This outing required me to be away from Stella for over 9 hours. Since her second teething was occurring, I would not be able to leave her free to roam the house, and I would be gone too long for her to be left in her crate. I called to ask if any of the Ladewig family members would be available to earn some money by dog-siting. Jennifer was ecstatic and said that it was an answer to her prayer. She explained that she needed to leave the house with another child for a long day of medical appointments and that Karis was too weak to attend with them, but she also was worried about Karis's emotional state. She felt that if Stella was there, it would be like having a guardian angel and a great distraction from any depravation Karis may be feeling.

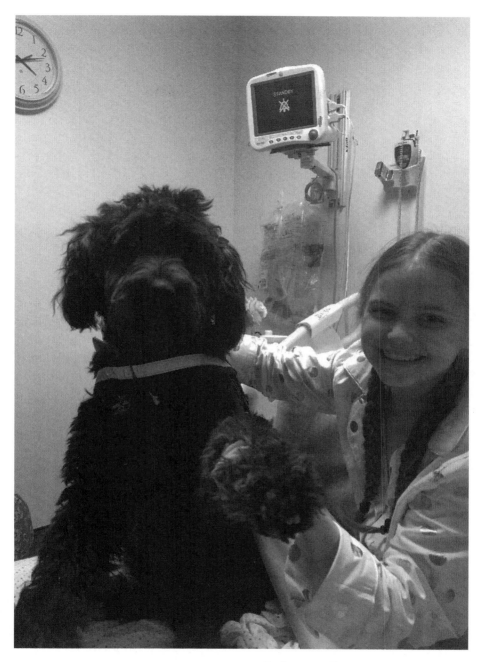

Stella visits Karis to brighten her day.

CHAPTER 5: KARIS

The day went swimmingly well, and again I found myself pondering how a service dog could benefit this family. I knew the emotional support dog part of it would be huge, but with them in and out of the hospital so much and the dad traveling, they would need a fully certified service dog who would be welcome to sleep at the hospital with the mom and two Total Parenteral Nutrition (TPN) kids during their stay. (TPN involves tubes that send nutrients straight into the blood stream, bypassing the digestive system altogether.) Kids on TPN are not typically eating, so therefore not in need of a food allergy detection dog. The children are not in wheelchairs or mobility impaired, so what act of service would a service dog be trained to do? And would I be able to find the resources needed to ensure the dog got fully trained if we offered up that option?

Most service dogs cost between $15,000–$35,000 when you consider purchase, feeding, lodging, medical, and training costs. So, I needed to be sure I thoroughly did my research before getting everyone's hopes up. I came up with a grand plan. I knew that Stella's parents had just given birth to a new litter that week. What if all the training put into Stella could be passed on from dog to dog, especially considering they came from the same parents? Could we train a dog faster to be a service dog now that we knew the new positive training techniques and had Stella to help us by modeling the desired behaviors? What if we could help train a service dog for the Ladewigs, of course with the help of a trainer as needed! What if we could bring in funds for the care and training of the dog with a book we all co-wrote!

Additional steps toward making this dream a reality came when I reached out to an organization I heard of through *Focus on the Family* called *Helping Hands*. They occasionally have funds set aside to address worthy requests, and I was able to connect them with the needs of the Ladewig family. It was so exciting when they agreed to help fund the expenses for the cost of the dog and the first two years of vet and food bills. And any extra training not included would be initially provided in housing and training from Stella and, of course, our family. Fabulous! Initial funds, a willing trainer (yours truly), a vision for additional financing, and this very deserving family would get a puppy trained as a community project and a book telling the story so that others could learn from the adventure.

Please donate to fund Mazie.

One exciting aspect of this new project was the idea of the whole family getting involved and united around something other than a health crisis. It took less than two weeks for all to realize that they indeed could have a dog and could take steps to be prepared for her to come live with them in due time, even if we could not get one with the same seemingly hypoallergenic coat as Stella. It was so exciting to watch expectant eyes light up when they started discussing who would have the yard clean-up duties or what gender they should get and listening to each one's position as to why their opinion should prevail. The prospect of a new puppy gave the entire family something to anticipate.

CHAPTER 6

MEGAN

MID TO LATE SUMMER 2017

My parents named me Megan Ladewig. I'm currently 11 years old, and I was born in Arlington, Texas. We have a large family: four sisters, one brother, and a cat. Well, we used to have a cat but had to give our cat away because some of us were allergic. This ties into many other issues our family has struggled with relating to adverse food/elemental reactions. The primary cause is a problem within our digestive system. That's led to many hospital visits and scares for our family, which can be stressful at times. I myself was born with a big fancy diagnosis called anaphylactic food allergies.

This was discovered when my mom fed me egg, and I started throwing up and broke out with hives. Another time at my sibling's school, there were trace remains of peanuts left on a table that I was playing on, and I reacted severely with shallow breathing, coughing, and again broke out in hives. This was the beginning of a series of incidents over the course of my life that involved countless doctor and hospital visits. We were told to try to build up tolerance for eggs and peanuts by exposing me to each in small amounts over a long period of time (desensitization). It worked with eggs but not with peanuts. This is all important because it led to meeting a close family friend that introduced me to a dog that didn't cause allergic reactions or problems for everyone in our family.

I was around 5 years old when we moved to the White Rock Lake area of east Dallas. I was excited but sad to leave the house that was so familiar. This new house was more accommodating for our family, although I had to share a room with my siblings: Karis and Phoebe. We are all homeschooled due to the intense and frequent medical issues/hospital stays, making it virtually impossible to stay caught up in regular school. Over the next couple of years, I remember spending long hours in the hospital multiple times due to severe, life threatening food or blood sugar reactions in my siblings. It has been a rollercoaster of emotions, but we've managed to stick together and help each other through it. I've found enjoyment in dance and different hobbies. My mom got us 6 fish that also served as a source of entertainment and responsibility to help us understand the nature of love and caring for another life. This was my introduction to pets and the major role they would eventually play in my life.

I've always been nervous around puppies because of their high energy and nipping. I was rarely around dogs growing up because the only dogs I knew at the time were my neighbor's and grandmother's dog.

Last year, my mother's friend, Miriam, asked my oldest sister, who was 20, to house-sit and watch her puppy, Stella. Since my sisters, Karis and Phoebe, again had to be admitted to the hospital for gut issues and my mom would be with them, I went with my remaining siblings and my older sister to stay at Miriam's home to help watch the puppy and their other dog, a yellow Labrador named Chloe.

When I first met Stella, the cute black 4-month-old Labradoodle, she jumped on me the second I walked in the door, and she bit me! Well, okay, she didn't do it on purpose but because she was excited. But still, it was not a great way to start our acquaintance! My sister suggested I go in the backyard and go on the trampoline with her, so she could burn off some energy. But this puppy is just way too crazy hyper for me! I ended up going on the swing just to get away.

Over the next few days, however, after playing more with Stella and working through my fear, I started to really love interacting and caring for this puppy. She was fun to run around with and seemed to have endless energy, but she eventually would exhaust herself and typically lay on one of the air vents on the floor. When I would relax and watch a dog show on TV, Stella would come over and lay on me. She was a cute little thing. Secretly, I always wanted a puppy but never considered asking for one because of all the effort involved and strain it could possibly take on a family with all our issues.

As time went on, I became friends with Miriam's daughter, Katelyn, who is one year younger than me. That meant that I saw a lot more of Stella. During this time, we learned that Stella was going to be trained as a service animal to help with Miriam's family's allergies. I had read about service dogs in books and *National Geographic* but never considered it being an option for someone I knew, let alone my friend. Whenever I would come over to Katelyn's house, I would watch Valerie and Miriam work with Stella and observed how quickly Stella picked up on her training.

Meanwhile, Miriam was observing my mom *light up like a Christmas tree* anytime she interacted with Stella when she'd come to pick me up from Miriam. Mom would get on the floor and play with the puppy for a very long time. She would transform every time she saw Stella—more peaceful, happy, and full of energy. This was exciting because with all the medical complications and Dad's work travel, as grateful as she was for her family, she was exhausted most of the time.

One day Miriam suggested that we should get a service animal for my sisters. My siblings and I of course fervently agreed, but Mom was hesitant, leaning far to the side of "no way." Mom felt it would be fun but doubted the family could handle the responsibility, and she certainly didn't need something else on her plate.

Miriam said she could get us one of Stella's sibling which we all thought would be super cool. Miriam sent Mom multiple pictures of a new litter of puppies. We also looked at the Novacek' (breeder) *Facebook* page, which had pictures of all the puppies and parents. My mom broke and decided she definitely wanted us to have a puppy but needed to talk to Dad. I think the most influential factor was that the puppy would be trained by Miriam and others prior to her coming to live with us as a service animal for our family.

After some persuading, Dad agreed to let us get a puppy. We responded with immediate excitement and began to pick out names for the girl puppy that we already had decided would be ours. It was going to be some time before we could see the puppy because of her age and training. We visited the Novacek' ranch twice. The first time my mom and Karis could not go because Karis was admitted to the hospital. This was also the time we decided to name her Mazie. Although we had a few other names picked out, we decided that she looked like a Mazie.

The second time we were all able to go. This was an interesting situation because one of the puppies bit through Phoebe's feeding tubing so most of my family packed up immediately to go home. However, I got to stay and continue visiting the puppies and then stay at Miriam's home for a few days with Stella and Chloe. By this time, I personally could not wait to get our puppy. After spending so much time with dogs, I was ready to watch our family grow and interact with our newest addition to the family.

Energy was ramping up because Miriam found out that she could bring the puppies home after an unfortunate case of ear mites ran its course. And then there was a bout with worms too. This delayed the process but increased our excitement while also giving us some good doses of reality as to what would be involved with raising a puppy. Dogs get sick too! Who knew?

I think the first time I really bonded with Mazie was at Miriam's lake-house soon after she came to live with Miriam to be trained. Going to the lake was super fun, especially because the dogs were there. Most of the time I was swimming and tubing with Katelyn or playing with Stella and Mazie outside. At the end of a wonderful day, Miriam dropped me off at my house and suggested Mazie come inside for a look at her forever home. The first room Mazie explored was the room I shared with Karis and Phoebe, which was cool because Mazie is going to work for Karis and Phoebe. It's like she came straight to the room where she'd be spending most of her time. Just a few months from now, Mazie will be our family service dog, trained to smell low blood sugar in Phoebe. Mazie will be sleeping in our room and spending almost every waking second with Phoebe, and I feel she already knows it. I can't wait!

CHAPTER 7

MAZIE MOVES IN AND TRAINING BEGINS

A few setbacks and a case of ear mites later, at 11 weeks, we were finally cleared to take Mazie home. We were so impressed that the Novacek refused to take payment until all health issues cleared. Quality breeder! This litter had been raised in a guest house and had visitors, but the pups had not been taken outside due to bad spring weather and differing set-backs on the ranch.

Now it was my time to shine, but I also knew that the window of opportunity to shape Mazie's response to stimuli closes between 12 and 16 weeks. So the operative word was MOVE! When you get your puppy, usually around eight weeks, having been socialized with the litter-mates, you want to make sure that you expose the pup to as many social situations as opportunities allow or you create. If possible, exposing your puppy to roughly 150 dogs is suggested. This can be difficult because you also need to wait on shots before going anywhere. In addition to interacting with other dogs, you want your puppy to know how to behave and react in a variety of circumstances.

I expose my puppies to loud noises at home and take them to the lake, local park, train station, downtown, or anywhere they can experience noises from items such as boats, lawn mowers, vacuum cleaners, helicopters and airplanes, or automobile traffic. Smells and textures are also equally important. An introduction to things like grass and other surfaces that we'll be walking on, helping the dog associate whether these surfaces are hot and cold, soft or hard, dangerous or messy. It's all about intentionality. My intention is to make all of these positive experiences.

Of course, you want to have an introduction to humans of varying ages and the odd things they carry such as umbrellas, strollers, wheelchairs, backpacks, or canes. These are things we take for granted but are commonly confusing to animals at first.

You want the dog to be comfortable in any environment or setting so that if your animal were going to be hunting with you, for instance, it would have already been exposed to the sounds of firearms.

If the dog is primarily to serve outside or might need to be near a lake or in water and on boats, you expose her to as much as you possibly can before you get too deep into training. Practicing on an unstable surface might mean that you hold your dog in your lap on a swing or put it in a baby swing at the park. I put Mazie in a little grocery cart or stroller and just let her feel what it was like to trust me. Taking my dog to the playground and letting her climb up the stairs and putting her in my lap while sliding down the slide will not only acclimate her to three-dimensional movement, but it also creates an additional learning environment to trust me. As the trust builds, she knows that I will only ask her to do things of which she is capable. Building that trust is more important at first then teaching your dog to sit. It's not just trust; it's also confidence in you and your techniques that you are building into your dog.

Planning ensures that you do not over-stimulate your dog. And for her own safety, be sure that your dog is never left alone while she is interacting with other dogs or people. It is crucial that you pay attention to and learn to read your puppy's body language. Are his ears going back out of fear, or is he leaning forward like he's ready to pounce and play? Conversely, when the stimuli overcome your dog, he must know that you will give him comfort and security. Please know that your dog will learn faster when he feels more secure.

We had to be careful to monitor Mazie's reactions to her situations and make sure she felt safe so as not to experience a lasting, permanent fear. This is especially true when in the company of other dogs. As soon as we brought Mazie home, we socialized her to our two dogs for three days and had the Ladewig family members come and visit.

As a part of my socialization protocol, I incorporate daily carpool trips to and from my children's activities. Our house is bustling with comings and goings of my kids and their friends, with their music and games. Fortunately the backyard contains a basketball goal and a hockey shooting pad, so the loud sounds of slap shots and balls bouncing occurred effortlessly. We were able to expose Mazie to unstable surfaces just as easily on the large round tree swing in our backyard and on the enclosed trampoline where my daughter would get a friend and roll a ball back and forth for her to chase while balancing. This exercise has been shown to increase trust and bonding as well as build the confidence your dog will need to preform many future service-oriented tasks.

So little time and so much to do. Keeping our socialization and sensory integration on track, we included Mazie at our annual Memorial Day lake-party. The sensory stimuli at the lake included:

- **Temperature:** hot sun on black fur, cool water.
- **Smells:** grilled food, fresh grass, fresh-caught fish, sunscreen, gasoline and exhaust from the water vehicles.

- **Sounds:** wind rustling leaves, jet ski and boat engines, lapping waves, music drifting over the water from nearby homes, people talking, laughing, and screaming.
- **Sights:** bright sun, shadows, lots of people and food, water toys, balls and waves.
- **Texture:** of wood on dock, fresh grass, hot concrete retaining wall, wet water, smooth fiberglass boat.
- **Taste:** food scraps being dropped and the perfume, sweat and or sunscreen being licked off people.
- **Vestibular:** input from the boat ride and being carried around by multiple people.

I would not recommend doing all of this as quickly as I did. If you were able to get the dog closer to eight weeks, you could spread out exposures and methodology. I was blessed with having the support of the other two dogs who were able to help show this puppy the ropes. Also, I wasn't exhausted because the entire family worked as a team, watching the puppy's body language for signs of stress. It was an immersion method of learning, but we relied on Chloe to provide a sweet, stable, and nurturing guidance. We needed Stella to exhibit a fearlessness and appetite for adventure. This combination gave Mazie a great balance for teaching her boundaries and encouraging her natural abilities.

CHAPTER 8

THE MAZIE PROJECT TAKES FORM

A fter the lake, while back in Dallas, we went to work on basic obedience. We were requiring Mazie to sit before being offered food, just as our other dogs do. Within a few weeks she had "sit, stay, lie down, and come." We decided it was time to take her for her first outing at the mall. Stella tagged along for coaching support. Arriving at the mall during what is considered "walker hours" (early before the mall opens), we outfitted both dogs with a GoPro camera and began their training while filming for a video documentary we hoped to add to our story. This was also Mazie's first opportunity for leash-walking as heretofore she hadn't had all her shots and was not to be out walking outside where animals like squirrels, rodents, cats, coyotes, and other dogs could carry or transmit disease.

To begin our training, we dropped a treat just inches from the dog's reach and commanded they "leave it," duplicating training we were working on at home. Next, we leash-walked them around to stores, took Mazie to her first restaurant, and walked around the second floor of the mall practicing commands she currently performed. She performed beautifully in this high distraction setting, reassuring me of the wonderful qualities being bred into the Novacek's Labradoodles.

A few weeks later, we progressed to Mutts Canine Cantina to help her socialize and fulfill the "150 dog exposures" that are suggested to make sure service dogs don't become aggressive.

One of the fun aspects about what we have come to call the "Mazie Project" is that my son's local high school friends were all able to gain school required service hours by joining us on training and filming sessions, which created a tight-knit community of volunteers. Within two months our team had expanded to include a film crew, a website developer, and social media expert—all interested in helping fund Mazie's future care needs. These young people were also a tremendous help with the endless games of find "Your Low" that we learned from *The Ping Project* Book (discussed in detail later). In this game, we would take saliva-covered cotton-balls and place them throughout the house and send Mazie on a search and reconnaissance mission to locate just these cotton balls. This interaction by the young folks gave them a new insight and a broader understanding of service dogs for invisible disabilities. I loved educating the young people about all aspects of what goes into training a service dog and watching their positive engagement and broadening acceptance, understanding, and empathy toward others. Dogs have a magical way of bringing out the best in humans.

CLICKER TRAINING

Because our window of training opportunity was shortened by about three weeks with Mazie, in addition to my acquired knowledge gained through training Stella, I chose to incorporate the program *How to Train a Service Dog in 30 Days* (*see resources*). This book focuses on "clicker" training and timing, which is essential to capture the dog executing the exact behavior you want naturally and then marking that behavior with a click followed by a treat. The very first step is conditioning or associating that the sound of the clicker is equals a treat and/or communicates that a treat will follow that click. This is done by thrusting a treat in the dog's mouth simultaneously or immediately following a click. In my opinion, this initial exposure is best accomplished with two people.

I wasn't a strong fan of clicker training to begin with, justifying that it was extra equipment to take along on outings and involved an additional training method to learn and implement. We were, after all, progressing well with voice only training. But I found that if I left a basket in clear view with treats, clicker, and the book open to the training of the day, I could implement these five-minute lessons into my busy schedule. By day five, I was sold.

Another benefit was that Stella also picked up on the clicker training. I introduced Stella to *101 Things To Do With A Box* (*see resources*) just using the clicker training. She was able to progress faster than I ever could have directed her on my own. As a bonus, I discovered that the clicker voices no emotion, unlike my voice, which may have conveyed frustration at times. Most importantly, Stella was able to figure out for herself the expected behaviors, allowing her to retain the knowledge for an extended period.

So, for each of the 30 days of training, I would initiate the activity of the day with Stella and have Mazie watch. Then, I put Stella up and repeated it with Mazie. Of course, Mazie did not get as far with the activities as Stella, but she sure came a long way rapidly.

As outings picked up we had members of the team film the body language of the dog and handler so that we could demonstrate how an ideal service team operates. A great team is so in touch with each other that they hardly notice the distractions in their surroundings. The dog should be frequently looking and listening for cues from the handler—or at least feeling for them from the other end of the leash. The handler should be checking for a change in the dog's demeanor: a sudden ear rise, extra yawns, unsettled restlessness, or any vocalization. If the dog should become fearful or stressed, the handler needs to immediately provide a reassuring touch and calming tone of voice. There should be plenty of opportunities for water, snack, and for potty breaks. A responsible handler will have a bowl, waste bags, treats, and hand sanitizing materials.

During the outings, we team members did our best to present working service dogs in their best light and educate the public when they had questions. However, keep in mind that many people using service dogs are just trying to get through their daily life, which is already difficult enough, and may not have time to field such inquiries. We choose to let the Labradoodles be touched if a passerby asks permission, and we have given the dog a "not working command" first. Doing so seems to help our dogs feel rewarded and focus better when back at work.

This might not be best for every team, so it is imperative when approaching a service animal that you note if the dog is wearing a vest with a patch: "Working, Do Not Pet." If so, please refrain from engaging the dog on any level. Otherwise, get in the habit of asking the handler for permission to touch the dog. Now that the scope of service dogs is expanding, some dogs have limited tasks that might include assisting with mobility. If their person is already seated and safe, they might welcome your inquiry to pet the dog. However, in the case of other services, dogs may be in service 24/7, and interjecting yourself into their workday might not be appropriate. In general, service dogs should be seen as medical equipment, and it would be unusual to ask to pet a wheelchair! Trainer Valerie is of the belief that dogs should be able to interact with the public at certain times during the day if that is what makes them tick. So, if you have a break time and can have a special command that lets the dog know he is not working, he may be petted. By all means encourage this.

CHAPTER 9

KATELYN'S EXPERIENCE WITH A SERVICE ANIMAL

Hello. My name is Katelyn. The reason I wanted to share my experience with readers is because my perspective as a 10-year-old is unique and atypical to any articles or books on service animals I have read.

Our family has had dogs my whole life. Although Bailey passed away a year after I was born, I'm grateful to have grown up with our dog Chloe. She is the sweetest yellow Lab who loves everyone and everything.

Mom and Dad put me in a social skills class when I was around eight years old. I thought it would be fun, but it wasn't. In the class we had two options: to play in the room or to play with the puppies. Mostly we would play in the room because some of the kids feared the dogs. But sometimes we would venture out to play with the dogs. We could pet them, hold them, play with them and their toys, and sometimes there was just one big dog. The big dog was trained well enough to play fetch with us. This was important to me because it highlighted my love for dogs and started what would become a lifelong desire to always want more dogs. This is what led to getting our next family dog.

When I was about nine years old, we got another dog after a long time of persistent begging. Her name is Stella Rosa! She is a black Labradoodle that my parents decided would be trained as a pet therapy animal. The goal would be for her to go into hospitals to provide comfort to my brother who became quite ill frequently, to provide love to children with terminal illnesses, and to provide for my personal safety by sniffing out raw egg whites, to which I'm highly allergic.

Stella went through training for an extensive period by one of the best local trainers. Beyond "sit," "down," "stay," "shake," "retrieve," and "deliver," Stella can actively participate in the household by opening and closing drawers and doors. During the first part of her youth, she was a service dog "in-training," which is not an easy task. Learning to be comfortable with bringing a dog into environments that they are typically not allowed is an adjustment. We trained in local dog parks, North Park mall, and Lowe's, and my favorite was when she came to see me at school lunch. It was interesting to watch her interact with the trainer and strangers in public. She is a food-centric dog and responds well to treats and positive reinforcement. Our trainer insists that positive reinforcement is the only way to go, and I agree.

After she graduated her course, we embarked on our first vacation where she would accompany us on an airplane to Beaver Creek. On the plane, she sat with my mother and did surprisingly well, even on takeoff and landing! Once we landed and arrived at our hotel, we took a stroll in the snow. It was her first time to see it, and she tried to eat it at first. She would shake off her legs and surprised herself when she sunk in deep. I had to laugh watching her play with a tennis ball. It was adorable because there was so much snow that when she stepped out to fetch she would sink right away. Every time she sunk it made me laugh a little in my head.

While in Colorado we went snowshoeing, and Stella got to load up on the Gondola with our entire family. It was fun watching her look out the windows while trying to figure out how she got up so high. I enjoyed climbing up the mountain and hearing the skiers talking about my dog. Stella has been a part of some of my favorite moments in the past year and quite the blessing to our family.

Realizing how much love she brings to our hearts, my mother decided she wanted to create an opportunity for our family friends to experience the same love and joy a service animal brought our family. Mom decided to get another puppy from Stella's original mother and father and train another dog to help our friends who have two children with life-threatening illnesses who have had Stella come visit them in the hospital before a scary procedure or during a long stay. My mom thought she had already put so much training into Stella that if we got a dog with similar intelligence and temperament, Stella would model many of her behaviors, and the puppy would learn from her, making it easier.

Our whole family was on board, and we decided that instead of a service-oriented mission trip out of the country this year, all our money and energy would go toward training another service dog. For my part, I help feeding and pooper scooping (not my favorite), but I do enjoy the puppy and am thrilled for my friend's family. I also went with Stella on the hospital visits and saw how much joy she brought to those girls. And even the nurses seemed to stay and visit happily.

Currently, we have three dogs in our home. It's so cool to take what we learned with Stella and apply all the learned tactics to our new little girl, Mazie. One of my favorite qualities about Mazie is her agility! If I throw a toy for her to play with, she will run after it and leap like a pouncing leopard! Of all the puppies I've been raised with, she's also been the softest, easiest to work with, and most trusting.

What I originally thought would be easy and fun has shown to be more than meets the eye. Raising a puppy is not easy. While there certainly has been fun, words like frustrating, awkward, exciting, and sometimes scary come to mind. The fun times typically surround taking Stella and Mazie out for walks up the street to the store or even to school. I enjoy the social interaction that accompanies having a dog. People can be different in backgrounds and social stature but bond over their dog interactions. Dog parks can be fun but scary because you never really know what will happen while you're out there. Because Stella got Giardia possibly from a dog park, I've been concerned about the upkeep of the park: dogs sharing water, etc.But at the end of the day, it ends up being just another part of raising a dog.

A funny yet awkward moment occurred one night when I was going to sleep. Stella jumped up on my back while I was on my knees and leaning over my bed and began exerting what experts describe as female dominance. When explaining this situation to my family, they couldn't help but laugh at my apparent distress and confusion surrounding the situation. Dictating this out loud is even funnier. Given that my mother is training Stella and Mazie to be service animals, we have been given many opportunities to experience all these emotions. We shoot videos, write stories, train in various locations, go on walks, dog parks, friend's houses, etc. There is never a dull moment with a puppy in the house.

And raising a service dog makes me appreciate the differences between our dogs and a regular pet, even from the same litter. Recently I went to the Ladewig house, and their eldest child came over with her dog Beau, whom happens to be Mazie's littermate. (She and her husband decided to get a dog too.) Now understand that Beau wasn't a service dog. He was being raised to be the family pet because that's what they want him to be. We were playing with him, and he nipped my ear! When I showed the adults, they said I should have schmucked him! Beau will have to meet a lot more humans and dogs before he can play well with others.

Stella turned into a smart and alert large puppy. She weighs about 70 pounds now. Mazie is still just a baby. She is in that fun stage where everyone thinks she's super cute and wants to pet and cuddle with her. Animals in general make me smile. Having animals that love me and allow me to love them are even better. And animals that make me smile, let me love them, and love me enough to help save my life are the best!!

CHAPTER 10

A MIDNIGHT CRISIS

ANOTHER COURSE CHANGE

Jennifer called me in tears, extremely worried. Phoebe's TPN pump malfunctioned, resulting in her blood sugar plummeting during the night to a mere 32 ml per deciliter. Had it gone much lower, the outcome could have been devastating. She said that by the grace of God, Phoebe woke up and came to her in the middle of the night in a cold sweat, crying, shaking and generally out of sorts. Jennifer immediately shot out of bed and identified the cause as a TPN pump malfunction, leading to Phoebe being deprived nutrition for over 4 hours. Phoebe can go a mere 1 ½ hours without TPN or IV dextrose before she feels her blood sugar dropping and the ensuing emotional upset that takes hours to calm.

Jennifer asked since we had not officially started to train Mazie on any specific service dog tasks for Karis could we assign Mazie to Phoebe for hypoglycemia detection? I knew we could train the dog but wasn't sure how that would affect Karis. And were we implying that one small pup could serve two very medically ill children? After prolonged talks with our trainer and team we decided to reassign Mazie as Phoebe's service dog, and since Karis and Phoebe spend much of their time at the same doctor appointments and share the same bedroom, Karis would still get the benefit of having a loving puppy in the house to light up her world.

In her service to Phoebe, our ultimate objective would be to train Mazie to detect hypoglycemia during the night hours as she slept. This would take some of the stress off Jennifer, who gets so little sleep and worries incessantly about her children.

You would think this would go swimmingly; however, Phoebe was very shy around dogs now, maybe due to having her TPN line bitten at the breeding ranch. She was usually the last one to come and sit down next to Mazie when they came to visit. She held back and was content just watching the others scramble over, and she never got into the squabble over who got to hold her or throw a ball to her or give her a treat first. Often, Phoebe passed on petting Mazie altogether. Time to get to work on empowering the new service dog team and training with Phoebe and Mazie alone without siblings.

To that end, Jennifer would bring Phoebe by our home for a visit, and I would implement games mostly derived from the diabetic alert dog training book *The Ping Project* (*see resources*) to help them interact and bond. Some of these games included hide and go seek where Mazie would have to sniff out Phoebe's scent. Phoebe began to warm to the little puppy.

Mazie learning to alert to Phoebe's low blood sugar in person.

During non-visiting days, we would keep up the training by having Mazie search for Phoebe's sweaty nightgown, which we kept in the freezer in a zip lock bag between uses. We also began to collect saliva samples by having Phoebe spit on cotton dental swabs and place them in a sealed glass jar, which we also stored in the freezer. To avoid contaminating the scent, we would pull out one swab using tongs and place it in Mazie's food bowl under a strainer filled with her food. This method helped to acclimate Mazie to the scent of the blood sugar range at which we wanted her to alert for Phoebe, which was about mid 60 ml per dcl. Later we learned thru Jillian (another allergen detection trainer) that breath on cotton balls gives a more accurate scent for the dog to alert to as the breath is what is most likely going to be accessible during sleep.

At this point I was so glad to have the extra help of all the high school students because Mazie was about five and a half months and starting intense outings, visiting the Dallas ZOO, State Fair, Aquarium, etc.—always with Stella in tow. We were in full filming mode and having two young dogs to manage was a full-time task.

These outings had a two-fold purpose. First, I needed to see that the dogs had operable behavior and could handle new and unusual situations, making sure that their prey drive would not overpower their willingness to work. Second, dogs do not generalize well. To have the best-trained dog, the service tasks need to be performed in every scenario possible. To that end, I would take along a sealed breath sample for Mazie to practice with while under distraction. At random times during the outing, I would put the sample under Mazie's nose and ask for a prompt alert indicating that anytime she smells that smell she needs to notify the handler, who would promptly reward her. While I was always focusing on prompt obedience work for low blood sugar detection, Mazie would need to be able to detect a change in Phoebe anywhere in any situation. She, unlike Stella, will likely have a "Working, Do Not Pet" patch on her vest once she is done training.

For Stella's training, I would bring a starch sample and a control sample and ask her to check them both before letting me know which one had the starch in it by alerting (pawing) that container. I would promptly reward her. For a dog to work consistently despite distraction, especially at these large venues, is a sure sign that you are making progress.

Stella guides Mazie through high stress outings like the State Fair of Texas.

CHAPTER 10: A MIDNIGHT CRISIS

CHAPTER 11

GETTING BACK IN THE SADDLE

An ongoing part of training with both Stella and Mazie has been the socialization of dogs to the humans they live with or will be living with. As time progressed, Mazie would spend more time with the Ladewig children, especially those she would serve: Karis and Phoebe. Everyone was on a learning curve as exemplified by this teachable moment as told by Jennifer Ladewig.

Many of the simpler training opportunities when Mazie came to visit were given to our girls to encourage some one-on-one time with the puppy and gain confidence in their ability to care for our new puppy. So, in teaching Mazie where it was appropriate to potty, Phoebe was often called upon to execute the task. On one such trip out to the backyard, Mazie spotted the next-door neighbor's dog. Phoebe tried to gain control of Mazie and get her to listen, but Mazie's attention was fixated on one thing: THAT DOG! Phoebe tried so hard to keep Mazie from exiting the backyard gate, but Mazie proved stronger and darted out the fence faster than lightening. Phoebe followed through mud and muck only to be knocked on her keister by an overexcited Mazie, who weighs the same as Phoebe.

I was beginning to worry a bit when the front door opened and in plodded Phoebe with Mazie in tow. Phoebe was sobbing uncontrollably. She was covered in mud, had a scraped knee and was clearly quite traumatized by the whole situation. I knew something had gone horribly wrong not only because of her crying and by the way she looked, but also because using the front door was so uncharacteristic! Slowly the story was recounted. I made sure Phoebe understood that Mazie did not mean to hurt her, and she just got a bit distracted and overexcited about seeing another dog. I reminded Phoebe that Mazie was only seven months old and was still very young. Just like her, Mazie had a lot to learn.

The next step was to get Phoebe back in the saddle so that she would not fear taking Mazie outside to go potty again. This was a bit of a challenge. We talked about how, just like kids, puppies are learning too, and sometimes learning is hard and scary. But we cannot fear it. We must get back on that horse, be brave, and just keep on going. We did have our back fence fixed so that Mazie could not be a little Houdini and escape again. This experience taught Phoebe as well as our whole family that as much as we train Mazie, she trains us too.

CHAPTER 12

LEARNING FROM STELLA

TRAINING FOR ALLERGENS

While I was training Mazie, Stella's allergen detection training was also taking shape. By this time, my son had been following the Specific Carbohydrate Diet (see *resources*) for digestive issues. This was proving successful in reducing hospital visits. Keeping him out of the hospital entirely was still the prime motive for training Stella. However, what I was asking Stella to do for us apparently had never been tackled—at least not published. The use of dogs in allergen detection is quite new—less than 10 years it appears—and gluten detection dogs have been in service under 5 years. I was told by the few experts whom

I could find that detecting all starches was just too broad a target for a dog to learn.

So, I narrowed my focus to the common hidden grains and starches that may be used as fillers, those that if ingested would send my son into intestinal distress. I am blessed to have an Institute of Integrative Nutrition health coaching and science background and a heavy interest in diet. For years, I had been following all the Paleo and super food trends, placing me in a position to decipher the technical lingo. I used that knowledge to settle on 13 top grains and starches. Ah, but how do we start this training?

Stella had accomplished alerting to wheat when presented as toast, a cracker, or egg whites (my daughter's allergen)—both raw and dehydrated. But I was stumped in how to proceed to trace amounts hidden in complex products like ketchup, salad dressings, or Twinkies, for instance. Fortunately, I was still in the research mode and was researching other service dogs and training. I found useful tips from the following resources *Super Sniffers*, "Willow Gluten Detection Dogs," "Texas Task Force Search and Rescue Dogs," multiple *YouTube service dog training* videos, and the *K9 Scent Training*. I also visited with *Allergen Detection service Dogs* (see *resources*). By studying each approach, I implemented combinations that made sense, even though most alleged gluten detection dog trainers were not encouraging. They felt that starch was too common a substance. Their reasoning was that my dog would alert to all plants in the back yard and food everywhere if I were able to isolate what they considered to be a truly universal starch sample.

I received a lot of feedback from experienced minds and ultimately ascertained that while what I was trying to do what hadn't been done YET, with the right amount of tenacity, I would succeed. If I can rationalize in my scientific brain that something is remotely possible, then I go solo, and keep going, with high hopes, to the best of my ability, never giving up. I analyzed why current training methods were not successful and then located another dog team that did similar work, including those who *were* successful in the search and rescue and drug sniffing realms. I'm very proud to say that with lots of games and fun, we were able to train Stella to identify all the scents required to be alerted to keep my son healthy. The combination of methods I implemented for starch allergen training delivered the results I needed.

In addition to the number of allergens we would introduce to Stella, another chief concern was whether I was "leading" my dog to alert subconsciously without her knowing for sure that the allergen was present. Several trainers and behaviorists in this field confirm definitively that I have achieved the alert response without leading.

In our training, to ensure the dog figures things out for herself, we borrowed tactics from the Diabetic Alert Dog training protocols with our own personal twist. All research we did indicated one smell at a time should be introduced for two months before introducing on another smell. We thought that that was crazy because we had multiple starches (13 to be precise), and we wanted the *same* alert for each one, just like we had seen done with bomb and drug dogs on all their instructional videos. The time it would have taken to train each individual starch would have been painstakingly tedious, not to mention my concern that Stella would get confused about what I was asking her if I kept changing and adding starches. I decided to train both simultaneously, taking the whole (all 13 starches), the parts, and combinations of each starch.

If I expected the same reaction to each starch, then I could train Stella for all of them at the same time. My thought was this: if I trained her for all the scents at the same time, expecting the same response, it would be easier for her to recognize all the illegal starches. However, I didn't want to confuse her by making her think that all 11 scents had to be present to warrant an alert. Imprint scent training occurs when the trainer links the scent to a reward in the dog's brain. Then, a word is attached to the command so that the dog understands what she is looking for in the future when the word gets spoken. They know what it smells like, search for it, and expect a reward for continued motivation, all of which inevitably creates a lasting memory imprint.

Remember: up until this point for starch alerts, we had been working with just an alert on toast, wheat waffles, or crackers. It was time to introduce something new. One of the more popular methods of training is the *Scent Wheel* (see *resources*). While it is a fantastic method, Stella didn't respond well to the training process. Somehow the large cans and the way we spun the wheel with a hockey stick made her extremely uneasy. This will make sense when you review the training found in *Super Sniffers* (see *resources*).

Stella actively trains with the Scent Wheel.

It was time to implement another creative approach via Miriam! We returned to a technique used in the beginning of Stella's training wherein treats were scattered about the house for her to search. I began by going to Whole Foods Market and putting together bags of various starches from their bins, including xanthan gum, corn starch, oat, rye, barley, wheat, quinoa, white potato, guar gum, rice, arrowroot powder, and tapioca starch. During morning feeding time, I put samples of ALL these starches in Stella's feeding bowl. Then, I placed a spaghetti strainer on top of this concoction and Stella's food in the strainer. For the evening feeding before she ate, I put together an Easter-egg-hunt type game in the backyard, representing each scent present in the morning feeding. Whole bags of the starch were hidden in the bushes and placed under patio furniture, behind trees. She was to "Search" or "Find It". I noticed that having the game outside was less stressful for Stella, and she was thoroughly engaged.

Stella locates starch hidden in backyard swing.

As time went on, I outsourced help from our team of high schoolers. I would have them hide mixed bags of starch in the back yard. Meanwhile, in order to ensure that we got her on film for a future documentary, I would keep Stella inside and distracted until I would give the command to search. Since she was SENT to search, it ensured that there would be no way I could lead her.

After we did that for a while and gave her a long two-hour break, we would bring the game inside and on a smaller scale. I learned from watching "Willow Service Dogs" on *YouTube* and checking out her site (see *resources*) that one protocol currently utilized for allergen detection included large, medium, and trace searches. So, to this end, I took a large piece of toast and sprinkled some of the starch powder on it. The toast was placed in a picture frame in the hall. Then, I had

Stella find it. Looking back and looking forward to future training, I could have just made a cracker by adding eggs with baking powder and cooking them. Another technique would be to add water, to the above mentioned starches and gums, mix well, and dehydrate in a dehydrator or oven until it becomes a wafer. For medium searches, we took a baby food jar and filled ¼ full with a starch powder combo. It was placed, for example, behind an open door near the kitchen, so she could not see it but had to locate it. After she succeeded at these two finds in short order, 45 seconds or less, I gave another break, and I moved on to ask her to search for trace elements. Now that she is proficient, I usually have her alternate the order of the finds.

It was time to tryout another game! What would happen if I took a piece of tape, dipped it in Stella's cocktail of starches, and then placed the tape somewhere in the kitchen for her to find? Then, I would mix two pieces of tape—increasing finally to four pieces of tape—and hide them around the kitchen for her to find. Looking back and having spoken with several more seasoned trainers, we could have gone a bit faster by not having her undergo so many searches at one time. Stella has a high food drive, and I would keep her in the game by switching out the treats during the game and by having several ways to play.

I introduced another parallel game with tape training that consisted of placing a spice in one envelope and loading another envelope with the same spice plus an added starch. Then, with one envelope in each hand, I would ask Stella to "search for starch" by picking which of my two hands had the starch. She responded very well to this training method, and I'd go as far as saying she *loved* this form of training. It was an extension of a game we played as a young puppy where we would hide a treat in one hand and have her pick. Eventually we added three envelopes: two with just spices and one with starch. This worked well because I could hold the envelopes in my hand between my fingers. She would paw at the envelope with the starch or try to bite it and receive an instant praise from me. We kept things interesting and engaging for Stella by alternating days. She trained with trace items first and large items last. This was followed by a day of large items first and trace items last.

At 16 months, Stella was getting 75% or more correct responses. I was asking quite a bit of her, but she responded so well and was happy in the learning. One trainer from Colorado said that asking for just two types of alerts, although seemingly simple, came at the risk of decreased accuracy. It is like writing the word red in blue ink and/or the word blue in red ink. It is simple to conceptualize but hard to carry out.

Stella allerts to plate containing offending allergens.

An ah-ha moment came in our training when I happened upon a *YouTube* video of people having their dogs check for gluten at the grocery store and alerting OR giving an all clear. I thought, "oh, now I have to teach an *alert and* an *all clear."* Jennifer helped me get the all clear down by suggesting Stella sniff a *zip-lock* bag of something other than starch and give her a treat associated with a new command. Her "all clear" comes when she sniffs the bag and there is nothing to alert to. She just looks up at me like I have lost my mind. Then I capture that look with click, treat, and I shape that response by calling it "all clear." Then I say, "good all clear." I proceeded to put a small portion of starch in a ziplock bag and asked her to "shake" (previously trained as a puppy during obedience training). Then the command was changed to "alert," and this progressed to "alert for starch". After she completed the task correctly by offering me her paw, I reward with her a click and treat, followed by the words "good alert for starch" in a high pitched excited voice.

As we progressed, we knew it was time to begin Stella's restaurant training. We wanted her to be able to alert our son for allergens in food he might order or buy away from the controlled diet at home. This proved a bit tricky for us because there was a recent blog in our local paper about dogs sitting in a booth with their human owners and eating at the table, posing as either service or emotional support animals. I was nervous that presenting a plate for Stella to check might be misconstrued as her sharing our meal. To overcome this perception, we went at non-peak hours, called ahead, and asked for a remote table with extra room for Stella to get out from under the table so that she could be beside me during all the food checks. We initially had the servers plate each item separately in a "to go" box, so she could only smell, not eat the food. We also asked them to bring little side sauces with added thickeners to have her check. She got five of seven correct on her first attempt, which is good considering dogs don't generalize well and she was distracted by the patrons sitting near us.

Once we progressed Stella to this point, I re-contacted Jillian, and she offered to guide me to the next steps. She refined Stella's previous alerts and added a different alert for eggs, *bow*, so she could alert for my daughter. Jillian reviewed the process for introducing a single allergen. With this knowledge, I could move to introduce each ingredient from our large starch mixture separately, allowing two weeks to train for each individual scent. However, to date, I have not seen the need to do this, but am assured I could implement these techniques if her accuracy regresses in the future.

Stella is currently 85–90% accurate with 13 trained grains and starches. Since service Dogs are considered medical equipment, an 85% alert is very high if you consider some of the medical tests and devices we use for detection. For example, mammograms are closer to 70% accurate and even give off false positives, yet are considered the gold standard in that arena.

Since we chose the "shake" alert for starch allergen alerts, a separate alert for eggs needed to be incorporated. Stella now "bows" for raw egg whites, "shakes" for starch she detects, and utilizes a calm stare while she ignores the non-threatening item as her "all clear" for all allergens.

It was time to see what this girl could do by putting it all together. It took four weeks to prepare Stella for her O.D.O.R test (see *resources*), designed to demonstrate accurate allergen training. In addition to the egg white, she alerts to not only the combo starches but also to taro root, soy flour, and flax seed; the last 3 she appears to have taught herself. Way to go Stella!

CHAPTER 13

CHRISTMAS BREAK 2017

T wo weeks before Christmas, I, Miriam, had a medical procedure and the idea of three dogs running under foot sounded dangerous. We decided to officially give Mazie over to the Ladewig family as an early Christmas present. They were ecstatic and enjoyed incorporating their new service dog in training Mazie into their daily routines, their regular HopeKids outings, and weekly doctor visits. All was going wonderfully well, and then Phoebe had to be hospitalized.

Mazie had her first real hospital experience when Phoebe was admitted on Christmas Eve. I came with Karis to ensure that Mazie had a positive experience and to watch for signs of being overwhelmed with the new surroundings. Emotions were running high as Phoebe and Jennifer were missing another Christmas at home with the rest of the family. Dogs can be very sensitive to these emotions, and Mazie bore watching closely. It was a pleasure to watch Karis handle the dog like it was second nature and walk confidently into the children's section of the hospital in order to introduce the family service dog to the nurses. These were the same nurses who just under a year ago had cared for Karis and had so enjoyed seeing Stella. Seeing this dream come to fruition within a year of conception brought tears of joy to my eyes. Mazie was clearly able to brighten Phoebe, calm Jennifer, and bring a bit of Christmas cheer to each of the nurses and doctors working the holiday shift. What a rewarding experience! A training bug and love for helping others in need was taking root. I am confident that any dog from Amy's litter will be quick to learn and have a demeanor that will ensure they never wash out of service dog work for either bad health or unfit personality traits.

During this holiday break, our own film engineer, Ilester, had an episode at our home wherein he dissociated and could not remember what had happened to his car or his belongings. Stella reacted immediately to Ilester's confusion and refused to leave his side. She stood at attention and let out a high-pitched cry as he moved about the house. Even when he needed the restroom, she stood outside the closed door, turning her head toward us for help and then back toward the door while continuing her whimpering. This lasted well over five hours with her not so much as lying down or leaving his side willingly, even to relieve herself. She had never behaved like this before, and we took note.

What was especially reassuring to me was that during the next encounter with Ilester, Stella greeted him heartily, jumping, vocalizing and licking him. But she quickly settled and curled up at my feet, letting us know all was ok; he was well. As luck would have it, the Novaceks had another litter of pups who were 6 weeks old at this point. And again I painted a picture of the future, asking Ilester to dream big and consider if a service dog might add a new dimension to *his* medical challenges.

DOGS IN VESTS

EARLY JANUARY

By January, Mazie was sleeping in her shared room with Phoebe and Karis, those she had been trained to serve. It had been Karis's turn to spend a week at the hospital, but she was home now, and the house was settling down to the new year. One night, soon after her return home, Karis awoke in the night to use the facilities and came face to face with a black Labradoodle, hovering over her, staring at her eerily. Had she been there all night? When Karis returned to bed, Mazie literally placed herself on Karis chest and licked her face. Mazie was alerting to Karis's condition! The next morning, she told her mom that Mazie was acting strange all night. Jennifer asked her how she was feeling, and Karis admitted she was not well. Her adrenal insufficiency was acting up, and off to the doctor they went.

Remember that Mazie had been trained specifically to alert to Phoebe's blood sugar and provide only emotional support to Karis. Mazie had alerted to Karis without any prompting or training. Not only that, but she proved she could wake up in the night to perform her service dog task. We are astounded that she is doing so much as an 11-month-old pup. We are now capturing and rewarding the extra alerting behaviors while making sure Mazie gets plenty of playtime and extra attention so that she doesn't burn out or worry excessively. We were intentional in our treatment of Mazie to prevent her from getting frightened that something scary will happen when she smells either of the girl's body chemistry off balance.

JENNIFER'S PERSPECTIVE: REAL ALERTS FOR MAZIE

Recently Mazie surprised us when she instinctively detected Karis having an adrenal crisis. Karis had recently been discharged from the hospital and was recovering from a serious staph infection, as well as dealing with two additional infections. On top of the infections, she was also recovering from two surgeries within a couple of days. When Karis came home from the hospital, she was stable and doing well. However, within a day or so, she contracted a cold virus and generally just wasn't feeling well. We assumed it was related more to her GI issues. Well, we were wrong. Mazie, sensing something bigger was going on, stayed up all night long alternating between sitting at the foot of Karis's bed watching her like a guard dog and either laying by Karis or on Karis, never leaving her unattended.

The next morning Karis told me what Mazie had done. You see, Karis has many health issues that have overlapping symptoms, and sometimes it is quite difficult to figure out what issue is causing the problem. Even though we had been treating her Addison's (a symptom of this disease is adrenal insufficiency) more aggressively, her body needed more steroid than it was getting. Due to Mazie alerting all night, I increased her steroid dose, and there was a dramatic improvement in her symptoms. I also noticed that Mazie was calm too. Dogs instincts are amazing! Mazie is not yet a year old, and she is already protecting and alerting to not only Phoebe's health issues but to Karis's as well.

CHAPTER 14

PUPPY PERSPECTIVE

Birth — Suddenly, I am pushed out of the small, comfortable space I have grown so used to sharing with my siblings. After spending so long in my cramped sanctuary, it feels so weird to not have anyone touching me. A pair of hands grabs me and wraps me in a soft material. I'm scared. I don't understand what is going on. I can't struggle against the fabric. I want to do something, anything, but I'm so tired. Finally, I surrender to my heavy eyelids. As my eyes close, I let everything fade away.

Senses — It's been a few weeks since I emerged from the womb. At least, that is what I hear some of the humans calling it. My eyesight, legs, and ears have been slowly developing. The world is so full of color and detail. When my ears were able to hear, I thought this world is *so* loud. I figured out that it was just my siblings. I am now able to walk and run just a little bit. I am waiting to see what else my body can do.

Meeting humans — I am lying down, having a nice snooze when five humans walk into my enclosure. For some reason, the humans start squealing. Can't a girl get a nap? The humans spread out, moving between my brothers and sisters. One of the humans picks me up and cradles me in her arms. She smells funny. Not bad. She just smells so different. I am not used to this smell. I do like this, though. Nestling my head against the human's chest brings me pleasure.

I hear the humans assigning names. One of the girls points at me and says, "We should name her Mocha." I scrunch my nose up at that name. One of the older girls says, "No, she should be named Mazie!" I am relieved that I will not be known as Mocha. But I sense it is time to get back to my nap! I walk straight into the lap of the good smelling girl. She cradles me in her arms, and my eyelids feel heavy. I haven't realized how worn out I am. Slowly, I fall asleep.

Play — I smell that my human visitors have again come to visit. I appreciate all the cuddling affection, but I want to play. The littlest human is wearing something on her back (a backpack). It is magnificent. Not only does it have bright colors, but it also has things hanging from it. I grab one of the green toys hanging from the girls back in my mouth. Tugging is useless against this strange toy. Nonetheless, I keep pulling on it anyway. I am joined by at least three of my siblings. The girl has something in her arm too, but it isn't nearly as interesting as the invincible tug-of-war toy that now seems to have a strongly delicious fluid coming out and into my mouth. The humans discover the leak, and three of them pack up and scurry away in a panic. I go to the corner and slowly fall asleep. These humans really take it out of me!

Pesky bugs — Recently, my ears have been itchy. I have also developed scabs on my head. My sibling and I are brought to the vet. As it turns out, we have ear mites. I don't know what that means, but now the person with the white coat says I can't go to my new home. When I get back to my mom, my siblings and I get a very yucky smelling ointment rubbed on our necks. We must do this every day for two weeks. I will be relieved when we don't need to use the yucky ointment anymore.

The Big Move Home — I am going to Momma Miriam's house today! A boy, I think his name is James, comes to pick me up. I am excited to see what my new home is going to be like but am a little sad to leave my brothers and sisters.

I am playing in my new backyard when five people come to visit, including two with the funny backpacks. I have a feeling these people are going to be important in my life. As I play with these humans, I notice each person has his/her own distinct scent. I play a little longer, but I think the humans can tell that I'm tired.

When they leave, I am sad to see them go, but happy that I can take a nap.

Mazie is tuckered out after playing with the Ladewig girls.

A little while after the visit from whom Momma Miriam calls my forever family, I am in my crate chewing on a bone. Momma Miriam throws in a squishy pillow. It smells like one of the girls who came to visit me. After I spend a little time smelling it, I decide that it is meant to be destroyed. I don't take my time ripping it apart either! When I am done, I admire my hard work. Then Momma Miriam throws in another squishy pillow just like the first, except this one smells like a different girl. I smell this one a while and decided to chew it up too. Now I have the scent of both girls memorized. I am guessing that these scents are going to be important later.

After a few months, I start what Momma Miriam calls scent training. I must sniff the breath of Phoebe, the youngest girl, and alert. I also must sniff her clothes. Those clothes smell different. It is not like her normal scent. There is something off about it. I can tell something is wrong, and that is why they want me to alert for this particular scent. I must do scent training several times a day. I get used to the smell after a while, and it is easier to alert.

Stella — I have a new friend, Stella. Well, actually she is my cousin and my new housemate. So, it is great to have a dog to tussle with in this busy human household. We sure love to play! One day we have a litter of humans come to the house with someone who smells vaguely familiar. It's Beau, my brother!! What a happy reunion I have with him! Well, at least it was for me! I jump on him because who doesn't like to wrestle? His eyes get huge, and he runs away. Stella and I keep trying to play with him, but he keeps running away. Honestly, I think he's a weenie. A few of the people get treats out of bags. Stella, Beau, and I run over to the closest human holding a treat. But to get a treat, they make us sit. I don't think that's fair. I do it anyway because I want a treat. I only get three treats. I want more, but they close the bag. Rats! The visitors don't stay long, and Stella and I find some really tasty bugs to eat.

Boats and other weird things — Yesterday, my new family brought me to a house that I've never visited before. In the backyard, there is a gate, and water is behind it. I hear people calling the big wooden platform/building a dock. Today a lot of new people came to visit. Everybody wants to haul me around. It's so hot! "Go put on Mazie's life vest." Two little girls approach me with the craziest contraption. It looks scary. It takes 10 minutes to strap me in, and in the end, I'm too hot and tired to care. If I had any energy and could reach the straps this baby would be long gone!

The big group arrives in something I don't recognize. It kind of reminds me of car, but I've only been in one of those a few times. It has a steering wheel, a window in front of the steering wheel, buttons and seats. I sit in the back with two girls. This whole situation makes me really nervous! The big, funny looking car starts up. It starts moving except we are on the water, not the road. There is so much wind, I can hardly see. My fur is going in every direction. The wind feels good because it is so hot outside, and I have this life vest on. I also feel little water droplets, not many though. Not a lot of water can get through my fur. I wish it could because it would cool me down.

After a while, one of the girls jumps out of the boat. "Girl overboard!" I'm just saying because I will not be going in after her. Looking back, there are three girls riding on a tube. This is information overload for my young brain. Retreat! I squeeze myself under the steering wheel table by the buttons. It is cooler under here. It feels so good to be out of the heat. Without the sun blazing down on my black fur, I just fall asleep. Before I know it, I'm being carried off the boat and I'm free at last. Let's just hope that's not a normal day in my new home.

Bug Delight — Even though I spend most of my days with Stella in the house where I am being trained, there are happy days and nights I spend with my forever family too, which is just a short car ride away. We're here! It smells so different here. This house smells like it hasn't had a dog in it in a long time. I can change that. Almost at once, three girls come up and hug me. I have seen these girls a lot lately when they visit trainer Miriam's home. Mamma Miriam encourages me to look around. So, I roam all over the house. It is a big house. I wander into a few of the rooms more than once. In the garage, I find a snack. More specifically, I found a big bug! It was delicious. The only thing is the floor tastes different from the floors at my other house. It didn't necessarily taste bad—just different. The girls aren't thrilled with my snack choice. "Oh Mazie! Please don't tell me you ate the cockroach! Oh gross! You did eat the cockroach! Mazie, gross!" The girl is yelling. I don't know why. The cockroach was delicious. I mean, come on. I'm a sucker for bite-sized snacks. A second girl freaks out too! I am so confused. Was I not supposed to eat it? Isn't that why it was on the floor? I walk out of the room. There is too much drama in there. My forever mom Jennifer calmly observes, "Come on, she's going to eat any edible object. Does a cockroach count as an edible object?" It does indeed! Lip smacking good. This Jennifer mom really gets me.

When it is time to sleep, Momma lets me cuddle and say good night to Phoebe and Karis. They smell like my chew pillows. I dream of tag, cockroaches, and treats!

Mazie — While I love training with Momma Miriam, I look forward to my forever family visits. I have missed the names they call me like Mazie Moo and baby. They also call me Mazie. It is weird how they say my name twice. I miss all the smells of the house and my toys. Oh, how I missed my toys. At this house, I can get bones and toys, and Stella can't take them away. My forever family gives me so much attention that sometimes it becomes a little too much. Sometimes I just want to lie on the cold floor. I don't know why, but I like to lie down on cold surfaces. I am showered here by hugs and love! What a lucky pup I am!

Carriage Rides and Nasty Beasts — Today, Megan, Phoebe, Karis, and Momma Jennifer came to my training house. Everyone except Momma is wearing a fancy dress. I jumped up on Momma because I am so happy to see her. As soon as I do that, though, everyone starts scolding me at once. When I get down, everyone stops scolding me and they say good girl. I want to be called a good girl again. So, I jump up on Momma and then get down back on all four legs. It happens again. As soon as

I get back down, I am called a good girl. I am about to jump up again when Momma grabs my collar and holds me down. Geez, this training stuff is tough! I still try to jump. I really don't think it's fair that I must wear a collar that they can use to pull me any way they choose! Karis and Megan are wearing collars (necklaces). They are a little too big for them in my opinion. But, I must say, they look quite majestic! We must be going somewhere fancy as I get to dress up too in my special vest. Of course, that means I'm working, but it can be fun!

We enjoy an evening of dinner (chicken!), dancing, and photo opportunities. It's time for a carriage ride, whatever that is. As we walk, I smell an animal. Then HE appears, a great, smelly beast! The beast is pulling what I'm guessing is the carriage. It is decked out in lights. I bark at the big beast just to make sure it doesn't have any ideas of getting close to Momma Jennifer. Momma obviously doesn't understand that I am trying to protect her because she says, "Mazie, no!" I growl deep in my throat, so deep, I don't think Momma heard. This thing is so scary; I just must bark and growl. Momma Miriam tells me that I cannot bark or growl at the monster. She says that I must get in the carriage and be a good girl. It takes all my willpower!

And this carriage thing is a nightmare! There aren't walls or even a whole floor to keep me from falling out. It smells bad. I lay down on the little floor. I don't want to move at all. I am afraid if I move, I will fall out! I spend the whole carriage ride waiting for that fatal turn to make me fall. Finally, the carriage stops, and I can jump out. I want to get far away from this big beast and its scary carriage as fast as I possibly can. In fact, if I never meet another one of those all the days of my life, that would be just fine with me! Momma Miriam says I need to be exposed to all types of creatures in life, but seriously!?

Playing Dress up — My forever family is always on the move. Today we go to a place that has a lot of people in it. Right away, I know that I will not enjoy this experience. First, Momma puts something with flowers around my neck and something sparkly on my head. I shake it off, but every time I shake it off, someone puts it back on. Momma, Karis, Megan, and Phoebe start dressing very silly. Then we stand in front of a big piece of paper, and someone with a flashing box comes forward. He couldn't be taking pictures. Pictures are taken on the small rectangles. I have no idea what this device is. The box flashes a couple times, and Megan takes my crown off. I am only putting up with this nonsense because I love my family.

Fortunately, we move outside where I get to go sit in the grass. I watch as people get inside these giant bubbles and run into each other. I do not understand the point of this game. It looks dangerous. I'm just glad that I don't have to do that! Just when I think all is well, Megan and Karis get inside the giant bubbles! Oh no! I watch them carefully. Surely they are not dumb enough to run into each other while wearing those bubbles. I see they walk backwards, and I am relieved that they aren't running into each other. I am confused when both girls turn around to face each other. Then I think, "Oh no! Don't do it!" And then they do it! They run as fast as they can and violently bounce off each other. I watch as they do it repeatedly. Karis eventually has a hard time getting up, and I can tell she is tired. They only bounce a few more times before they get out of the bubbles.

Karis sits down with me and she is panting (I mean breathing) hard. I keep her company as she catches her breath. Out of nowhere, a man in a bubble comes half rolling, half bouncing towards me. I back up as fast as I can. I can't go very far because Momma Jennifer is holding my leash. Squished by a giant bubble—what a horrible way to die! "Get away, get away!" I try frantically, but Momma and Karis assure me all is well, and today is not the end of me. "It's ok," I hear over and over. If it weren't for all the humans that love me, this world would be one big scary place for this little puppy!

Vet Day — Today, I went to the vet. The vet laid me down on a big table and gave me a shot. It hurt just a little bit, but in just a moment everything fades from view. I was out like a light. I wake up with something around my neck, and it is SO big. I am not used to this thing around my neck, but it definitely is NOT the collar I came in with!

Crazy Cone — This morning I wake up, and I remember that I have the crazy contraption around my neck. I did find out one thing—this thing around my neck is small enough that I can itch my belly. My belly has been so itchy ever since I woke up at the vet yesterday. So, I start to itch, but something isn't right. Then I realize what it is. I'm completely naked down there. When did this happen? As I am trying to figure out what to think of this horrifying situation, Momma Jennifer yells at me and says, "No itching." She says that she must go get an even bigger "cone of shame." I remember the big cone I had yesterday before Momma Miriam put the smaller one on me. I couldn't even lay down without it getting in the way. Momma tells me to sit up, but I am determined to not have that cone around my neck. It looks like Momma is about to give up. I am ready to celebrate my victory, when Momma shoves that cone over my head. I am not happy at all right now. After the cone is on, I lay down on the floor and think about how unfair life is.

Every time I go potty, it is a struggle. I try to sniff to find a good spot to do my business, but I keep stepping on this terrible cone. I bet those humans didn't think about THAT angle! It is so annoying! Finally, I just must settle on a spot and make do.

I can't even play with my toys or chew on my bones. This cone won't let me. It's evil. What am I supposed to do all day? I am in the living room, looking longingly out the window. I see a squirrel right next to the window. My belly might be a little sore, but that is not going to keep me from jumping on the windowsill. Karis says, "Mazie, no!" But Momma Jennifer says that it is ok. I jump down and look around the room for an open door, but there are none. I want that squirrel so bad—so bad that I start to cry. "I just want the squirrel! I'm not asking for much. Just let me out to catch the squirrel." Everyone just says things like, "Aw, Mazie." It sounds like they feel bad for me, but they still won't let me out! I just don't get it. A dog and her cone—I hope they are soon parted.

Mazie wants a squirrel.

Breath Alert — Momma Jennifer is trying to get me to smell Karis's breath just like when she has me smell Phoebe's breath. The scent is familiar, yet it's also different from anything I have smelled so far. The fact that Beau is in the other room is not helping matters. Momma Jennifer tells me to alert, but this is not the scent that I have been trained to alert for. She lifts my paw and has me paw Karis. I'm confused. Am I supposed to alert for Phoebe and Karis? Am I changing the scent I am alerting for? After a while, I think Momma Jennifer can tell I am confused because she lets me go and play with my brother. Still, I have the feeling that new games and treats are in my future!

CHAPTER 15

THE VALUE OF EMOTIONAL SUPPORT DOGS

I n our personal journey of dog ownership, our training goal transitioned from therapy to service, but when it came to Mazie, her tasking included an emotional support element. Our book would not be complete unless we included a mature perspective of the value of an emotional support animal, as this training might be the path our readers may take, given the rigors of service animal training.

VICTOR'S STORY

Hero was the first dog I ever experienced really loving. My friend introduced me to this loving creature one night when I arrived at his parent's house to hang out and watch movies. I've always loved animals, so the instant connection was no surprise. Little did I know that this dog would become the foundation of a spiritual revolution and kindle a passion for dogs.

I'll be honest; I grew up with cats. Mother always told me that she felt a dog would be good for me. "A boy and his dog," she always said, "I'm entirely too busy for a dog. They require too much maintenance and walks, etc. Dogs are drama."

Secretly, I just never believed I possessed the structure and advanced humility it would require owning a dog. Remaining cognizant of a dog's needs —walks, feeding, vet visits, shots, boarding, grooming, and any additional needs—can be a lot to take on for someone who doesn't have patience, resources, and organization.

While hanging out with my friend on a consistent basis, I was able to enjoy a lot of moments with Hero. Hero was a mix between malamute and German shepherd. Beyond his aptitude and loving nature, the dog is simply beautiful. He has long, flowing hair and a big bushy tail.

Eventually I moved into a large apartment with my friend and his dog. Since I didn't expect to ever live with a dog, I wasn't exactly certain how this would go. Typically, my living space is incredibly clean, free of dust and especially hair. The only long-term interaction with dogs I'd had up this point was with three pugs owned by my aunt. As much as I loved these creatures, they snorted, stunk, were hyper, got all up in my business, and required more attention than I did—immediate competition.

My work ran from 10:00 A.M. to 6:00 P.M., Monday through Friday, but my roommate was up and out of the house much earlier. Assuming morning responsibility of Hero surfaced as a major highlight of my day. Remember, he is a big, fluffy, German shepherd-malamute mix. As a kid, I loved wolves, so getting to live with a dog that looked like a wolf was right out of my fantasy world. For the longest time, I woke up, ran around making coffee, breakfast, obsessively cleaning, and darting out to run some errands for my client before getting into the office. During these mornings of hurry, I noticed Hero would follow me all around the house, watching me prepare for my day.

On certain mornings, I would be up early enough to fulfill my morning rituals of prayer, meditation, and a daily scripture reading. Next, I would collect Hero and head down for his morning walk. But, frequently I'd be rushing due to new morning orders from my boss or unexpected events. That being the case, I'd have to leave Hero in the apartment and head out for the day. I really noticed how attached I had become when uncharacteristically I began enlisting the help of neighbors to walk Hero. I remember when I first started to care. I remember the moment in the car thinking, "Oh gosh, I would hate to have to go potty and not be able to do it for an entire day, let alone having to deal with the repercussions of getting chastised when my owner finally came home for going in the house if I had no other option."

And so, it began: an opportunity to get outside of myself and focus on another life. It was an extremely eye-opening experience. I realized at that moment that owning a dog was a lot like raising a child. I had to consider his needs before my own, to make sure he was taken care of before I could rest and relax, not in a codependent way, but in a loving, parental way.

Everything after that seemed to unfold cohesively as I got to work early and began my checklist for the day. It was the beginning of a new way of operating and the beginning of an incredible appreciation for my four-legged friend.

We underestimate the relationships that come in the form of friend or animal. Hero was a beacon of unconditional love and always trusted the adults in his life to foster his livelihood. I will always remember what Hero did for my life, habits, prayer life, and inevitably he birthed the desire to get my own dog after my roommate and I went our separate ways.

The concept of Emotional Support Animals had been brought to my attention by a friend who got a dog and had me help her name it. She was going through an incredible amount of pain from the end of a relationship, trying to self-medicate herself into oblivion until enough time had passed that she didn't have to feel anymore. The adoption of that dog was essential in her ability to find light at the end of a dark tunnel. One day she was heading to travel to her family's ranch and was unable to fly on her family's plane to get there. I asked what she was going to do to get her dog on a commercial flight, and she told me that her dog was "prescribed" to her and was in training to be an emotional support animal; thus, he could travel with her without complication.

She was the first to recommend this form of therapy to me. Ironically, I had gone through a lot of the same stuff she was going through from a traumatic break up, to my family moving away, and a complete lifestyle change that would remove any form of visible or current safety nets from my path. In other words, it was a dive into adulthood, a break from childish ways, and the ability to grow into the man I knew I could be apart from the expectations of my family and the world. So much happened in a short period of time that, as usual, I didn't give myself the time to heal. I jumped right in to starting a business, leaving a full-time job that I loved, and trying to muster up the confidence to be the person my business mentor demanded I be.

While I was fulfilling the role, I felt hired to play. I began to grow exceedingly less confident in the direction I was heading. I had built up resentments on top of fears that started to hinder growth in relationships, both personal and vocational. Everything became an evaluation of people's character, as determined by me, and an avoidance of introspection. In other words, the wall was up; people were not going to get in, and everything was strictly business. Trying to play both sides of a sensitive yet totalitarian individualist, I deprived myself of the emotions and creativity that once fueled my altruism and connectivity to people and the world around me. I started to compartmentalize and file away anything I considered to be negative. If I buried it and didn't acknowledge it, then I didn't have to talk about it, or so I thought.

I remember being extremely depressed. I had just moved to Dallas into a situation that I considered less than desirable. The only advantage was that I would be surrounded by what are now my closest friends in the entire world, with access to opportunities to be of service unparalleled to anything I had ever experienced. But all of that was yet to be revealed.

It was a short time after moving into the apartments that I put almost everything, from work to dating, on hold. Don't misunderstand me; I was still working with people in various service opportunities. But what I would not do is let people speak truth and love into my life so that I could start the process of mending pieces of my broken life.

Fortunately, I had a new friend who needed my help. Anna and I set out one day with intent to find her employment and to check out some puppies I had been researching. What people did not know was that I had been researching bringing a dog into my life for months. After multiple e-mails, visits, research on dogs online, and consideration of which would be a perfect fit for me, I found a litter of puppies on *Craigslist* that needed to be rescued from an eventual transfer to the pound. The family, who already had two mature dogs, had welcomed a littler of 10 puppies but could not afford the medical requirements of raising each puppy even from 6 weeks old. It was serendipitous in the sense that Anna and I discussed not going to see them due to the tight schedule we had set for the day. After all, the puppies were 42 miles away, and we each had evening plans. But after a short deliberation, we turned up the music, put the windows down, and decided we would just casually visit without making any purchases.

When we got there we quickly noticed the both the dogs and the puppies were living outside, in conditions much different from the Ranch that bred Stella and Mazie. I had dreamed of getting a fully American Kennel Club (AKC) certified pup, and these living conditions were not what I had envisioned.

I was torn between holding out for my fairy tale pup and wanting to be a hero by rescuing a puppy. I was also nervous about the less domesticated puppy becoming a terror later in life. I was looking for a wolf hybrid puppy. I've done extensive research on wolf pups and how their personality relates to humans. All I can say is I loved everything about them and wanted the challenge of raising one to be loyal, loving, and emotionally bonded.

No harm in looking, right? Walking back to the area where they kept the new pups, I was instantly enamored. They were making the cutest little puppy sounds: infant versions of howls. I sat down with my legs crossed and started to observe each puppy. Feelings were welling up inside of me, and I quickly realized this was not going to end the way my friend and I had discussed. These wolf pups were exactly what I was looking for: Malamute and Husky—wolf mix. In other words, the perfect puppies! I shut my eyes and prayed fervently. If I was going to make a life changing decision to be responsible for a life, I had to get God involved.

Disappointingly, none of the puppies seemed to respond to me sitting there, singing soothing words, and petting them as they grazed past. They were cute and adorable to pick up, but they didn't do anything out of the norm that said, "I choose you." That was my goal. I wanted the puppy to choose me.

I saw one little loaner puppy sitting in the corner. The owner pointed to him and said he was her favorite. He had the longest tail and possessed the most wolf-like qualities. He appeared to be the runt of the litter, but she wasn't exactly sure. I looked at him and said, "Hey boy, okay?" He leaned his head back upside down, and his little squinted eyes barely opened as he gave a guttural wolf puppy howl. And what eyes he had! One blue and one brown! "Here boy," I encouraged, and he trotted over with a pathetic but endearing stumble. He got right inside my lap and curled up, resting his face on my calf.

That of course was the moment I had been waiting for, the moment where I received a sign that he was the one. I thought that I was going to be putting him back down and coming back to get him a few weeks later, when to my surprise, his owner said, "Great, he's yours! Y'all can head home together today if you're going to take him to the vet and begin all the necessary medical care."

DOGS IN VESTS

Feelings of excitement and elation swept over me while I was also feeling mildly nervous about the new life that I had just taken ownership to parent, and parent well. Then again, this was the moment I had been waiting on for years! I knew my patience had paid off. All my tenacity, pragmatism, and discernment had pyramided to this moment. I held the little guy in my hand less than 3 inches from my face. He licked my nose. I got up, left quickly with my sweet friend, and began life with this new and special creature.

I named him Malachi. This was done for no other reason than the name was brought to my mind. I looked up the meaning; it meant messenger of God, and I loved the spiritual implications. Thus, I decided that would be his name. There is also an old Indian legend that animals with Heterochromia (two different colored eyes) can see the spirit world as well as the human world.

About the time I purchased Malachi, I took on a new client, Miriam, whom shared in the joy of my new puppy. She encouraged me to bring him by the house on the days I worked for her and her family. At the same time, she purchased Stella, her beautiful Labradoodle, from the ranch previously mentioned and was putting her through top tier training program under Valerie. Valerie was incredibly kind and gave me some great pointers during the raising of my puppy.

One of the best contributing factors to his current demeanor was the amount of time I was able to spend with him in his first year. Not only did I get him at six weeks, but I was fortunate enough to only work a couple days of the week outside of retainer items for my clients. Two of the days I worked at a dog park in uptown that served gourmet food and craft cocktails. My close friends owned and managed the dog park, and it would ensure that I could take Malachi to work with me, while monitoring (and monetizing) the time I got to spend ensuring Malachi was well-adjusted and socialized with other dogs.

My primary reason for getting a dog, whether I realized it at the time or not, was to have a companion. By taking a year to focus on service work, the lives of others, my current client base, and odd jobs that would connect me with community in Dallas, I began to settle into a comfortable rhythm. The biggest social glue in my entire life was the existence of Malachi. So many friends came out of the woodwork to be a part of his life. My friends would just show up to hang out with my little wolf pup. I worked at a local athletic- ware store that was heavily involved in the community and provided free access to gyms internationally. They also allowed me to bring my pup to work. Between this job, my client's welcoming homes, and Mutts Dog Cantina, Malachi was able to accompany me everywhere.

A new acquaintance introduced me to the idea of certifying Malachi as an emotional support animal. To be candid, I originally wanted to take her up on asking one of my many friends that were doctors to "prescribe" me an emotional support animal so I could avoid transportation fees, and take him anywhere without being questioned. When I got into a deeper conversation about the true nature of an emotional support animal, I found that she had been prescribed an emotional support animal that, in turn, helped her navigate away from the many prescription medications she was taking for anxiety and depression. Although she still takes one medication (as opposed to the 14 she had access to), her primary source of improvement is focusing on something other than herself, which from all indications has taken the place of medications.

This is not to say that all Emotional Support Animals can replace medication. But there is a strong possibility that the animal can be utilized as an alternative, or in addition to medication, depending on each person's situation and the precise recommendation of a medical professional. From that perspective, maybe Malachi really is an emotional support animal. I certainly felt more balance in my life, more settled and calmer. When I reflected on my lifestyle changes after adopting him, what was most prevalent was the changes being made to accommodate the dog's schedule.

My schedule started with going to bed earlier and getting up earlier. I had to learn the dog's routine so that I could avoid the many messes in my home. I also had to plan the time for him to play and grow, socialize, take naps, and kennel train him. I spent many hours training him to do the basics—sit, stay, lie down, shake, and high five. He also knows how to speak (which is the most adorable little wolf howl) and stays close by my side on and off the leash (but never comes off leash in public). He listens to my call if he's far away and comes running, and at a little over two years, he has made it out of the kennel and can roam freely around the house while I'm gone.

And all lived happily ever after. Wrong. I cannot leave out the trials and tribulations that occurred during the early phases of his life. It was not an easy road. The most growth I've had in my life occurred during that first year of his life. Malachi taught me the value of time; the lack of value in material things; the importance of companionship; the power of touch, self-sacrifice, patience, and protection; a glimpse into being a father; and finally the art of community in raising an animal.

Victor and Malachi take a nap.

I remember when Malachi was a baby, and I woke up in the middle of the night to the smell of excrement. The most adorable fluff ball was curled up in my arms; next to him was a pile of poop and large urine stain. The stink was heavy, and the damage to my down comforter and duvet was evident. I remember being incredibly frustrated, primarily because I woke up at four in the morning and had an important client meeting at eight in the morning, for which I wanted to be mentally prepared. Add in the mess and cleaning my linens to avoid permanent damage—I was over the top. I angrily took him to the bathtub and washed him under the faucet. To this day, my dog is not a fan of water. It could be simply because the breed has a natural aversion, but I can't help but think that it's because of the vigorous washing experience that could have scared him and made him fearful of water. While it's primarily showers that bother him, he will run out of the bathroom sometimes when the sink is turned on loudly or the shower turns on. I'm slowly acclimating him to the noises and loving him through the fear, but it's a strong reminder that in dog training, all our actions have consequences that can last a lifetime.

Our animals must be nurtured. This process is a huge steppingstone in what I believe is the leveling of my pride and character defects that get in the way of God being useful in my life. When I focus on Malachi and raising him properly, I'm not thinking about me and everything I want. It's an interesting scenario. In fact, it's an incredible scenario. I could not have anticipated that my impulsive decision to adopt a dog would have a significant impact on my life, to the degree that I started to grow spiritually and emotionally. Now the thoughts that go through my brain are "okay, the linens can be cleaned. It's not that big of a deal; if they need to be replaced, I can replace them. At the very least I can go to the dry cleaners." Nothing is worth uncontrollable anger toward what I considered my child.

Having that mindset prepared me for the days I *thought* I could leave Malachi out of a kennel in my absence. The mayhem I came home to was incredible. Couch cushions removed from the sofa, holes dug through the lining, trash strewn across my apartment, the buckle chewed off my designer belt, and the worst, a hole dug through my memory foam mattress and my sheets on my side of the bed. There are more damages that have ensued over the past two years, but this was ONE moment that will live for me forever, mostly because of my reaction. This was a day that I was trying to live off no sleep and people pleasing. It was a perfect storm that I walked into this mess. I thought I was handling everything in stride, coming to terms with all the damage until I saw my bed. When I noticed the bed, I was furious! Malachi and I had many a word, and I took him downstairs with me and tied him to a railing while I had an intense conversation with one of my buddies who is a counselor that was working nearby. I tell the reader this because again, dog ownership is not all rainbows and unicorns. I've had nearly everything considerably important to me of material value destroyed in some capacity: shoes, belts, beds, and my car.

Victor and Malachi discuss rules for the car.

Oh, the car. That situation was entirely my fault. This is also important to notice because with dogs, it is always our fault. It will never be their fault. Animals do their best to train us how to behave with them; however, it is up to us to listen. There is nothing an animal can do that I haven't allowed to happen in some form or another. Malachi trained me quite quickly that leaving him in the car (while it was running, of course, with the air-conditioning on) for even small amounts of time (like while I handled a traffic ticket) was not okay for him. He chewed up my emergency break and scratched the glass portion of my gear shifter. These were two very expensive chew toys. They were like that designer belt.

I remember getting in the car and laughing at the damage because instantly, as both Miriam and Valerie would reassure me later, it was my fault. All the previous scenarios led to this point of acceptance. It was such a blessing that I could smile in the face of that adversity. Why? Because through this creature, God was able to remind me that a life will always be more important than a thing and that things, no matter what their worldly value, were never important to being with. Thanks to Malachi for being the vehicle in which I could learn these truths.

So yes, I was a self-absorbed, materialistic, flashy, guarded, fearful, people pleasing mess of a young adult that was desperately seeking a fast turnaround. Malachi has bridged the gap from my emotionally jaded, harrowing spiral into depression, self-preservation, and confusion to the confident, open-minded, hard worker I've grown into today. More importantly, the vault of my heart was reopened, some would say reoriented, to let light and love back in again. Maybe that would have happened eventually, but maybe it wouldn't. What is important is that I'm emotionally available again. I can speak out of the overflow of gratitude in my heart because I strive to focus on what I'm grateful for versus what I think I need. Malachi is a piece to the puzzle of relationships and life that has become a new foundation for how I interact with friends and family. There will always be a dog in the picture. The dog is not the missing link, but the dog is the conduit or vessel that reminds me of God's great love for me and that everything will be okay. Just as important, he's shown me how to care deeply for something outside of myself, regardless of my external circumstances. He's laid right next to me as I've grown in the life of my prayer and meditation. More than anything, I've laughed so much more, slept better than ever, and loved effortlessly.

He truly is an emotional support animal, and yes, he was prescribed by my psychologist. I recommend therapy for anyone. The best possible combat against depression, anxiety, addiction, etc. is a bio-psycho-social approach. If you are an animal lover, I strongly recommend utilizing an emotional support animal in tandem with a strong spiritual journey, a strong community or support group, and if necessary, the operative suggested by a medical professional.

CHAPTER 16

YOUNG ADULT PERSPECTIVES

While training a service dog comes with a myriad of blessings and wonderful outcomes, the fact remains that these animals are most affective when bonded for life to those they serve. Adapting and embracing this service is an adjustment, however, especially when your disability affects you as a teen or young adult. We've included several forthright perspectives that the young adult family members and volunteers felt should be considered.

MASON'S PERSPECTIVE

Most people enjoy having an animal and the attention it brings with it, so what better than a service dog trained to lookout for you and you alone. Okay, so yeah, the dog is cool, and people are excited to see it, but there are some unwanted associations.

For me, a dog, especially one clearly labeled "service dog," brings unwanted attention. When you enter a room, people immediately single you out, and suddenly you become the center of attention for all the wrong reasons. Someone might think, "That guy that must have some kind of issue." This creates anxiety in others and me, and it leads to isolation and separation. It can be much harder to make close friends in larger groups. And to some extent, your companion serves as an albatross around your neck. Do your friends have dog allergies? Is there room in the car? The service dog is just one more thing to worry about when are trying to fit in. Just go about your business. The needs of the dog must constantly be considered as well. The most relatable experience I can think of is the exercise your health teacher gives his students to carry around a pretend baby for a month; at the end of the 30 days you wonder if you'll ever want children. Dogs begin as puppies—wild, crazy, puppies!

Service dog training is EXPENSIVE. My parents could have paid for a car or paid off my medical bills if they hadn't chosen to owner train. If you train them yourselves, an awful lot of time goes into that training, and you risk taking away from family time, even if your end game seems worth the sacrifice. Of course, if someone else trains your expensive dog, there is the chance that they never will bond to you, the owner.

One of the scary aspects of a service dog is that while 75% accuracy sounds great, this is my life we're talking about! The tendency is to relax and let the dog take responsibility for my health. But let's face it, they're not perfect.

So, while I see the value of our service dog, please take into consideration your young person's receptivity before you jump in with both feet into this expensive and time-consuming enterprise. Just sayin'.

ILESTER'S PERSPECTIVE

While working with the intelligent service dogs (Stella and Mazie), who are Labradoodles, I often wondered how a third service dog, who I will be naming Otto, would benefit *me* through this journey we call life. Being a millennial who battles a mental health issue and that is on daily medication, I could see that owning a service dog would be helpful for me personally. His alerting me to take my medicine as well as keeping me active outdoors while I considered his needs for exercise would enrich my life. We would be a true team; I would be dedicated to the care and training of my teammate, and Otto would help keep me out of the hospital. Service dogs are trained to put their owner first, but I think putting my service dogs needs before my own would be a key part of our relationship.

Jay and Amy Novacek, who have taken their time to breed these beautiful dogs specifically to become helpers for people in need of a devoted, loving animal would provide the pup. In the future, I envision that *my* family would bond over my amazing dog Otto, even my dad who isn't that keen to have a pet in the house. I anticipate that once he sees an attitude change in me and a change in the direction of my mental health that he too would see that this service dog meets all his expectations.

I have been involved with these pups this last year, and I have seen the wonderful and amazing tasks these Labradoodles have accomplished and done right before my eyes. I am anxious to get on my own path to training. Miriam and Valerie have challenged their dogs, and the outcome is astonishing. A goal of this project, which includes both filming—which I was a part of— and this book was to raise proceeds in order to cover expenses for raising Mazie and future service dogs. I would feel privileged to have a dog trained for me by this team in the coming months.

I am so convinced that a service dog would benefit me and others who suffer from similar mental health issues that I am willing to step out of my comfort zone and share my story, however difficult that is for me to put into words and print. Raising awareness of what these wonderful dogs can do for young people who suffer from invisible disabilities is my prime objective. I hope that I can continue to be a part of service dog training on multiple levels in the future. I will be healthier and satisfied knowing that others with disabilities, both visible and invisible, can be helped by my contributions.

JAMES' PERSPECTIVE

The moment I get home, there she is. The beautiful Stella is running, bounding, and slobbering all over the place. The way that these dogs recognize their owners and are filled with joy to see them really helps make a house feel like home. Even after I have been away for months, when I come home, Stella will jump up, put her paws on me, and go crazy. While this is just a small thing, it will be something I always look forward to when I come home. Having an animal that cares about you can change the way you see her. Yes, it helps to bond with your adopted animal early, but being around the dog makes him aware of your particular moods and behaviors. Most of the time, the dogs (if you are on a regular schedule) will know what time you normally come home at the end of the day and will be waiting for you by the window or by the back door to greet you with full on, unabashed excitement. They may even pee because they get so excited.

James bonding with Stella the day she came home. He let her sleep in his lap for over an hour so as not to disturb her.

CHAPTER 16: YOUNG ADULT PERSPECTIVES

CHAPTER 17

FINAL THOUGHTS

We hope you found this book to be an entertaining and informative overview of our path to training service and emotional support dogs. Here we are at the end of our tail, pun intended. We are waiting to see if Stella will win a Guinness Book of World Record category for detecting the most allergens; her application has been submitted. We should know the Status by August 2018.

Mazie and Malachi are on course to pass CGC this Spring, so stay tuned and follow us on *Facebook page 'Dogs* in Vest' or our website www. dogsinvests.com.

But it doesn't end for you. It is your turn to go forth and bond with your purchased service dog or decide if a future dog could bring fulfillment and blessing to your life. You service dog could be one who is looking out for your wellbeing possibly with better accuracy than current medical equipment. Undeniably, there are some extra costs and time spent on training—and definitely extra chores—but they are so worthwhile. The healing relationship of a great team is a gift for all to experience.

For all dog owners or would-be owners, all our resources both mentioned and not mentioned in our previous pages are below. Please use and share them freely because a well-trained dog is a gift to all. Thank you for allowing us to share our heart and passion with you. We look forward to hearing YOUR story, so please reach out and share with us on our *Facebook* page and our website.

WWW.DOGSINVESTS.COM

Please donate to the $501(c)(3)$ on our site to sponsor Mazie's care and training. This is our website that tells the story of Stella, Mazie, and Malachi and all who helped to train them. Please follow our progress and sign up for our newsletter for updates. This beautiful story surrounds the eclectic lives of a family, their friends, and astute service animals that work and provide

For those who love numbers the statistics for the Ladewig girls medical upkeep include the following:

- 10 injections a months
- 4 port accesses a month
- 4-8 laundry basket sized boxes of medical supplies delivered each week
- 3-10 medical appointment a week (average is 5)
- 2 kids that are TPN dependent requiring IV medication multiple times daily

APPENDIX

EXPLANATIONS & ELABORATIONS

The Importance of Team Training

We believe you achieve the best results while training your own pet or dog because you've learned to read your dog well. You know its body language when something is not right. You observe the nuances in its responses to games, requests, distractions, and other dogs. You cannot make these connections if you simply drop your dog off at a trainer and picking the pup up in five months! Allowing others to train your animal, and not being part of that team, puts you at a huge disadvantage. Bonding, trust and confidence need to come gradually from the moment the decision to own a dog is reached. That is why we encourage the family to pick their dog from the breeder. While we are the initial trainers of Mazie, the forever family visited frequently—as much as twice a week—to ensure connection and observe progression. By witnessing the training process, the forever family gains confidence in their ability to model future training.

Finding a Trainer

We found our trainer, Valerie Fry, owner of Canine Solutions in Dallas, through the Park Cities Animal Hospital here in the city. But an animal behaviorist might be another resource. It is not easy to locate a local service dog trainer. But we have found *The Ping Project* book extremely helpful for D.A.D.'s training, and Debbie Kay also has a DVD program called Super Sniffers (website referenced above), which we found helpful. I also reached out to Jullian Skalky of *Creating New Tales* (website referenced above), but unless you live in Florida, she is only able to board and train your dog herself or communicate via Skype.

Training Guidelines

We try to train the dogs five days per week in short sessions throughout the day, usually at least 3/25-minute sessions for obedience and public access.

Duration Distance Distraction: An Explanation

Dogs do not generalize, and a concept learned at home does not naturally translate in the grocery store or park, so we train each skill in all variety of locations. We use the concepts of duration, distance, and distraction.

If we initially ask the dog to "stay," we reward the behavior quickly, after 2 seconds. The duration is then increased in 5-second increments until a two-minute-stay is achieved. Next, we work on distance. I back away 5 feet and then another 5 feet as she masters her stay at 15–20 feet from the trainer. Then you want to add distraction to the mix. When you are at home, this could be the doorbell ringing or a toy that I toss and catch in the air while the stay command is requested. Once we master these commands in the house, we move to a different location in the house and then to the backyard and eventually to field trip locations.

Is Service Animal Training Right for You?

In considering this undertaking, make sure you can afford the expense and the investment of time to properly train your service dog. Taking an extended leave from work to train might be a strong consideration. It could be the difference between having a best friend for life and having an animal that just lives with you. It is important to find a trainer who will give you a lesson plan (roadmap to get to your end goal). Do the research yourself if you can't locate a trainer. Watch videos on *YouTube* or movies to become more informed about what tools are available to train your service dog. You need to honestly test your puppy's mental abilities to learn and retain information. You need to ideally spend 15 minutes per day on brain exercises, but remember that your puppy needs to sleep for 3 or 4 hours at a stretch as they tire easily. After nap time, you need start the training again. This cycle repeats throughout the day.

Pet Therapy Information

There are some very stringent requirements for an animal to be considered for pet therapy opportunities. One of the first steps is to register with a therapy certification company like Pet Partners (www.petpartners.org) while beginning the training process. This will not be quick and requires months of training while adhering to their strict guidelines.

Some of the rules are as follows:

1. The animal must have a bath within 24 hours before working and be well groomed.
2. The animal must not be on a raw food diet.
3. No visits are to last more than 2 hours. (During this time, it is the handler's primary job to search for any signs of stress in the therapy animal. He or she must then appropriately defuse any stress or tension to ensure no accidents or behavior could be deemed aggressive by the uneducated public.)

RESOURCES

www.hhmin.org

This is the 501(c)(3) that is accepting the funds from the donations we raise and from the sales of this book to help with the care and training of Mazie and any future service dogs we train.

Stratton Ladewig

sladewig@csntm.org

Stratton is an experienced editor and served as a grammatical editor and secondary copyeditor for this book. He earned both his Master of Theology and Doctor of Philosophy from Dallas Theological Seminary, where he focused his writing in the area of New Testament Greek grammar. His work has been published in the reputable journal, *Filología neotestamentaria*. He currently serves as the Project Manager for the Center for the Study of New Testament Manuscripts and as a chaplain for the U.S. Army Reserve.

Linda Savage

lindasavagecpc@gmail.com

Linda was immensely helpful for helping all the writers find their voice and organizing the project for flow and relate ability.

Linda provides services as a freelance copyeditor and proofreader for debut authors to enhance clarity and readability. Linda is a Certified Professional Coach, educator and public speaker with a BA from the University of California Irvine. She makes her home in Gilbert, AZ.

Brian Hare

www.dognition.com

This is an awesome site used by Duke University that Brian Hare developed. Dognition helps the owner understand how their dog learns through simple tests, resulting in better training experiences for both the dog and trainer. We had Stella perform these tests in April of 2017, and she scored in the ACE category. This knowledge helped me change up her treats and training style to refocus her interest on the task being trained.

Amy Novacek

Novacek's 84 Labradoodles

Novacek's 84 Labradoodles is on *Facebook*. We are excited to connect you with our breeding partner, Amy Novacek, who produces smart, gentle, and successful service animals.

Amy Novacek
Canine Companions
http://www.equinechronicle.com/
canine-companions-help-owner-amy-
novacek-compete-at-apha-world-show/

Valerie Fry
www.caninesolutionsdallas.net
Valerie is a graduate of The Karen
Pryor Academy of Animal Training
and Behavior. Valerie is a Certified
Level 2 Dog Trainer for Animal
Behavior College. She is a Mentor
trainer for the Animal Behavior
College, CATCH Canine Trainers
Academy, and The Victoria Stilwell
Academy. As a Professional member
of the Association of Professional
Dog Trainers, she actively pursues
the study of canine behavior and
modification techniques. Valerie is
also a CGC Evaluator and C.L.A.S.S.
instructor and evaluator.

Dawn Scheu
www.willowceliacallergenservice-
dogs.com
Dawn has one of the first trained
gluten detection dogs and has
helped to pioneer the Bergen
detection-training world. She has
contributed greatly by co-developing
the O.D.O.R. test that Stella passed
under Jillian for raw egg whites.

Jillian Skalky
www.creatingnewtails.com
Jillian provides various levels of
training from boarding and training
your animal to remote Skype sessions.
She is the trainer we consulted
to proof Stella on a single scent.
She is also a co-developer of the
O.D.O.R test. Located in Hollywood,
Florida, Creating New Tails provides
dog training services specializing
in personalized dog training for
service, assistance,and alert dogs.

Donna Hill B.Sc. (zoology) B.Ed.
Donna Hill Dog Blog
Training service dog tasks since
2007, Donna is recognized globally
for her two YouTube Dog Training
channels and her "VI Assistance
Dog blog."

Debbie Kay
Debbie Kay Super Sniffer
Debbie is the author of Super
Sniffers and developer of the scent
training wheel we tried to use with
Stella. Debbie K Super Sniffer Scent
Wheel we referenced is from this
handbook.

Leah Sullivan
Ultimate Guide to Dog Training
Training Your Own service Dog: Step by

Step Instructions with 30 Day Intensive Training Program to Get You Started. Kindle Edition

Patricia B. McConnell, Ph.D.
The Other End of the Leash
This is a book that focuses on how we can significantly impact the way we interact with our dogs by understanding life from their perspective.

Stewart Nordensson and Lydia Kelley
https://www.amazon.com/Teamwork-II-Training-Manual-Disabilities/dp/0965621618
This is a wonderful dog manual for people with disabilities that helps them train their own service pet! The second edition is a revised copy that goes more in depth on specific training procedures.

101 Things to Do With a Box
www.clickertraining.com
This online library contains a treasure chest of articles, brimming with timeless training tips, how-to techniques, and ideas. To keep these article gems in circulation, they share them monthly. Try *101 Things to Do with a Box* to provide some mental stimulation for your dog during long winter seasons.

This classic training game and boredom-buster was first introduced by who else?: Karen Pryor! This training game is derived from a dolphin research project in which Karen Pryor and others participated: "The creative porpoise training for novel behavior," published in the *Journal of Experimental Analysis of Behavior* in 1969. It has become a favorite with dog trainers.

***The Ping Project* Shari Finger**
www.thepingproject.com
Diabetic alert dogs can detect when a diabetic's blood sugar level is too high or too low with amazing accuracy (often 10–20 minutes before their blood meter). The Ping Project proves that diabetic alert dogs can be trained at home without the need of a professional trainer with only the cost of having a dog in the household. Follow step-by-step how a family with a ten-year-old boy with type 1 diabetes trained an abandoned puppy as a diabetic alert dog, and the dog is now his best friend and faithful companion.

Lucky Dog Barkery

www.theluckydogbarkery.com
Lucky Dog Barkery is the kind of store your dog would build. The Dallas brick and mortar store is a premier shopping experience for dogs and their owners. I want to extend a special thanks to the helpful staff (Kierin Stevens, Ben Pratt, Erika Davila, Braden Parrish, and owner Marsha Lindsey not shown), who pulled products with and without starch before I arrived, so Stella could blindly check for starch, ensuring I was not leading her alerts.

www.bbonze.net

Billi Bonze provides high quality grooming services. They also have a fun boutique filled with toys and treats for dogs. We are thankful for the great grooming services and the service dog discount.

www.petpartners.org

Pet Partners is an association providing training, testing, and certification for therapy animals.

Ciara Gavin

www.allergendetectionservicedogs.com
Ciara Gavin, owner and certified dog trainer, was very generous with her explanations of the new field of allergen detection and gave references with examples to medical equipment accuracy comparisons.

Leerburg Institute

www.leerburg.com
The Leerburg Institute is a family owned and operated business that focuses on quality training and top tier products. The equipment they sell is designed and used by professional dog trainers who are out in the field every day. The training material they produced is by trainers and is based on techniques that they implement every day.

Texas Task Force 2

texastaskforce2.org
The Texas Task Force team provided insights on seek and find techniques.

Elaine Gottschall

Breaking the Vicious Cycle is a comprehensive book on the Specific Carbohydrate Diet.
http://www.breakingthevicious-cycle.info/p/where-to-buy/

Shannon Eavenson

Gut Feeling; Gut Healing is a wonderful uplifting resource incorporating the Specific Carbohydrate Diet and lifestyle management for those with chronic intestinal illness.
https://www.amazon.com/Gut-Feeling-Carbohydrate-Nutrition-Lifestyle/dp/1543118747

Resi Gerritsen, Ruud Haak

Detection Dog (K9 Professional Training Series).
https://www.amazon.com/Scent-Training-Identification-Detection-Professional/dp/1550595849

Tim Hawkins YouTube Video on Krispy Kreme Donuts
https://www.youtube.com/watch?v=NAlvaZzq23k

Jana Rade is the creative director of impact studios, esteemed author of *Symptoms to Watch for in Your Dog*. She also created the cover of our book!
www.impactstudiosonline.com

Training Locations
Mutts Canine Cantina
Northpark Mall
Lowe's
Home Depot
Hollywood Feed
Petsmart
Yolk! Restaurant

ABOUT THE AUTHORS

MIRIAM RICHARD

Miriam Richard earned a bachelor's degree in kinesiology with a minor in psychology at the University of Texas, Austin. She went on to receive a master's degree in physical therapy from the Texas Women's University in Houston. She was then awarded a health coaching certification from the Institute of Integrative Nutrition.

She has been happily married for twenty-four years, and Miriam is the mother of three kids and two wonderful dogs. She resides in the Dallas/Fort Worth Metroplex. In addition to her work and ongoing holistic research, she writes educational and therapeutic songs to pass her knowledge on to others. She enjoys taking on projects wholeheartedly and is full of passion for helping other. She is currently working on a dogumentary for *Dogs in Vest* and planning a training video series with the help of Valerie Fry and team members.

Miriam and Stella bond.

VICTOR FADOOL

Victor Fadool operates a lifestyle manager business in the Dallas metroplex. Victor caters to local families and the complex lives they lead. Serving in the privacy of his clients' homes, he works in tandem on various projects throughout the DFW area. His involvement with Miriam Richard as a client led to the birth of a business that will bring service animals to the lives of families with various struggles. They seek to provide proper training methods as well as inform the public of the adequate resources they need to succeed. Additionally, they have worked side by side to get her dog, Stella, into the Guinness Book of World Records for most scents alerted by a service animal. Victor's wolf-dog, Malachi, serves as an emotional support animal. Malachi has come to be known and loved in the community and provided love and support for various men in recovery from addiction.

KARIS LADEWIG

Karis Ladewig is TPN dependent, and she uses books to escape reality. Allergies and eczema keep her inside a lot of the time. Despite these chronic illnesses, she has always been able to take joy in reading and writing. Karis has dreamed of becoming an author, so naturally she was ecstatic when Miriam Richard asked her for help in writing a book about her beloved service dog, Mazie. Karis is often low on energy, so helping to write a book was a productive past time for when she had to lay low. She loves writing from the viewpoint of animals and objects, which is how she approached her contribution to this book. After this book is published, Karis will continue writing, and she will wait to discover where this passion of hers will take her.

Made in the USA
San Bernardino, CA
28 July 2018